get COOKING!

with

The best recipes from *This Morning's*
Brian Turner and Susan Brookes

BCA

LONDON   NEW YORK   SYDNEY   TORONTO

This edition published in 1996 by BCA by arrangement with HarperCollins*Publishers*

CN 4617

Text © 1996 Granada Television Ltd
Photographs © 1996 HarperCollins*Publishers*
Stills from THIS MORNING © 1996 Granada Television Ltd

A catalogue record for this book is available from the British Library.

For **This Morning**
Creative Co-ordinator: Helen Williams

For **HarperCollins*Publishers***
Editorial Director: Polly Powell
Commissioning Editor: Barbara Dixon
Production: Bridget Scanlon

Designed and produced by SP Creative Design
Linden House, King's Road, Bury St Edmunds, Suffolk IP33 3DJ
Editor: Heather Thomas
Designer: Rolando Ugolini

Photography
Food photography: Bruce Head
Food stylist: Steven Wheeler

Colour reproduction by Saxon Photolitho, Norwich, UK
Printed and bound by Lego SpA, Vicenza, Italy

CONTENTS

Introduction 6

CHAPTER ONE

Traditional Food & Family Favourites – 10

CHAPTER TWO

Snacks & Fast Food – 24

CHAPTER THREE

Supper Dishes – 38

CHAPTER FOUR

Budget Meals – 54

CHAPTER FIVE

Vegetarian Food – 68

CHAPTER SIX

International Flavours – 82

CHAPTER SEVEN

Entertaining – 98

CHAPTER EIGHT

Desserts and Puddings – 116

CHAPTER NINE

Cakes and Baking – 132

Index 142

GET COOKING
INTRODUCTION

We never thought on that exciting, terrifying day eight years ago that *This Morning* would still be here so many programmes later – and still essentially the same. There wasn't time to think of anything

except being ready for the next item, as it was a mad scramble to get on air for such a long time in a new studio, despite the weeks of preparation. I remember trying to assemble a salad into something that looked appetizing on the studio floor in among the camera cables – we had forgotten to ask for a preparation kitchen, and the worktops were being used by Andrew to set up as a hairdressing item!

Somehow we got through those first programmes, even if we were a little ragged at the edges in those early days. The viewers seemed to forgive us our mistakes because it was obvious, then as now, that if something goes wrong on live television you have to make the best of it and carry on. It's amazing really how little has gone disastrously astray. I can recall the finished dish ending up on the floor only once, when our guest cook was Sherry from *Coronation Street*.

I once went to the oven to say, "This is what it will look like after baking", opened the door with a flourish, and there was nothing there. And I'll never forget the morning I was cooking four poached pears in red wine, and Richard ate one of them when he was feeling a bit peckish

and so it had to be three poached pears. However, I'm not the only one with problems. Turning things out seems to be a problem for Turner – I'll say no more!

The food on This Morning is always real and edible, not because of some great decision from the Boss, but because the crew eat it. After such an early start, they're starving by mid morning. We used to think that food items were popular because everyone was interested in cooking, but our crew is more interested in eating. They are quite fussy about the choice of recipes, too, and

often offer suggestions. Bruce on camera five is a great foodie and I value his opinion. Ian who takes the top shots from a camera up the spiral staircase, doesn't like fish because the smells seem to collect up there in the studio ceiling.

Of course, our choice of recipes is influenced by the team as well as the viewers. I always know that Judy will like seafood, the girls in make-up often want something vegetarian, Richard will eat anything except garlic ice cream, and the sound department are somehow always there when there's wine from Charles.

In this book, we have tried to give everyone a taste of something they will enjoy, from those on a budget to someone who is trying to impress dinner guests. Many of the recipes may be old favourites for regular viewers who have written in for them in their droves over the years. Others may be new to you – perhaps you missed a day, or a guest cook presented some new exciting flavours or a classically superb dish.

With this book in your hands and seeing us all have such fun in the kitchen, there's no excuse for anyone not to get cooking.

Susan Brookes

CHAPTER ONE

TRADITIONAL FOOD & FAMILY FAVOURITES

Even though we now eat a more international and varied diet, we can still enjoy traditional food cooked in the old-fashioned way. The recipes in this chapter are just a small part of the British culinary tradition and which have become firm family favourites.

Creamy Fish Pie (see page 13)

BEEF COBBLER

A cobbler is traditionally made with a scone topping, but when time is short, why not try topping it with hunks of French bread instead? Simply spread some generous slices of baguette with garlic butter, then pile some grated cheese on top and pop under the grill to toast until bubbling. Serve the dish with buttered and peppered seasonal cabbage.

1 quantity Tasty Meat Sauce (opposite)
50g/2oz butter
1-2 garlic cloves, crushed
1 small French bread stick, sliced
115g/4oz red Leicester cheese, grated

1 Preheat the grill. Make up the Tasty Meat Sauce and, while it is piping hot, pour into a large casserole dish.
2 Cream the butter until softened and then beat in the garlic. Spread the garlic butter over the slices of French bread. Arrange on top of the sauce.
3 Sprinkle the grated cheese over the bread and place the cobbler under the hot grill for about 5 minutes, until the cheese is bubbling and golden brown. Serve immediately with a green vegetable and more French bread to mop up the delicious sauce.
SERVES: 4

QUICK CRUNCHY COTTAGE PIE

Peeling, boiling and mashing potatoes for a cottage pie can be time-consuming, so why not try an alternative to creamed potatoes? Simply use a packet of instant mash.

1 quantity Tasty Meat Sauce (opposite)
1 packet instant mash
2 tablespoons chopped fresh parsley
salt and freshly ground black pepper
1 tomato, sliced, to garnish
2 sprigs parsley, to garnish

1 Preheat the oven to180°C, 350°F, Gas Mark 4. Make up the Tasty Meat Sauce and transfer to an ovenproof dish.
2 Make up the instant mash according to the packet instructions. Mix in the chopped parsley and salt and pepper to taste. Pile the potato mash over the meat mixture and level out with a fork, but don't press down too much.
3 Bake in the oven for 35-40 minutes, until the meat mixture is bubbling and the potato is golden brown. Serve garnished with sliced tomato and sprigs of parsley accompanied by seasonal vegetables.
SERVES: 4

CUMBERLAND SAUCE

This wonderful sauce can be stored in the refrigerator in a screwtop jar as a useful standby.

2 oranges
5 tablespoons redcurrant jelly
150ml/¹/4 pint port
1 heaped teaspoon mustard powder
1 heaped teaspoon ground ginger

1 Pare the rind from both the oranges and cut into thin julienne strips. Place the strips in a basin and cover with boiling water. Leave for 5 minutes to soften, then drain.
2 Put the redcurrant jelly and port in a saucepan and heat through gently, stirring to dissolve the jelly.
3 Blend the mustard and ginger with the juice of 1 orange to a smooth paste. Stir into the port mixture and continue to heat gently.
4 Add the drained julienne strips. Leave to cool, then store in a screwtop jar in the refrigerator until required.
MAKES: 175ml/6fl oz

CREAMY FISH PIE

450g/1lb white fish fillets, skinned and cubed
225g/8oz shelled prawns
1 x 300g/10oz can sweetcorn kernels
40g/1¹/₂oz plain flour
300ml/¹/₂ pint white wine or cider
40g/1¹/₂oz butter, flaked
1 teaspoon anchovy essence, or French mustard
4 tablespoons double cream
salt and freshly ground black pepper

FOR THE TOPPING:
115g/4oz chopped mixed nuts
115g/4oz oatmeal
115g/4oz grated cheese
1 tablespoon chopped fresh parsley

1 Place the fish in a lightly buttered ovenproof dish with the prawns and sweetcorn kernels.
2 Make the sauce: put the flour and wine or cider in a small saucepan over gentle heat, and whisk in the butter. Continue whisking until the sauce is thick and smooth. Boil for 1 minute, then remove from the heat and stir in the anchovy essence or mustard, cream, and salt and pepper to taste.
3 Mix well and then pour the sauce over the fish mixture.
4 Make the topping by mixing the topping ingredients together, and sprinkle evenly over the dish.
5 Bake in a preheated oven at 180°C, 350°F, Gas Mark 4 for 30 minutes, until crisp and golden.
SERVES: 4

75g/3oz red lentils
2 medium carrots, sliced
115g/4oz mushrooms, sliced
2 tablespoons Worcestershire sauce
2 tablespoons tomato purée
¹/₂ teaspoon mixed dried herbs
300ml/¹/₂ pint beef stock or red wine
salt and pepper

TASTY MEAT SAUCE

2 tablespoons vegetable oil
1 large onion, finely chopped
1 garlic clove, crushed
115g/4oz streaky bacon, rind removed and chopped
350g/12oz good quality minced beef, lamb or pork
1 x 400g/14oz can chopped tomatoes with herbs

1 Heat the oil in a large saucepan and add the onion and garlic. Cook over gentle heat until softened but not brown.
2 Stir in the bacon and mince, stirring with a wooden spoon to break up the mince. Cook gently for 3-5 minutes until the mince browns.
3 Stir in the tomatoes, lentils, carrots, mushrooms, Worcestershire sauce, tomato purée and herbs. Season with salt and pepper, and add the stock or wine.
4 Cover the pan and simmer for 40-45 minutes, stirring occasionally, until the mixture is cooked and has thickened slightly. Serve with potatoes or pasta, or in the relevant recipes in this book.
SERVES: 4

SAUSAGE CAKES AND HERBY TOAD

2 eggs, beaten
300ml/¹/₂ pint milk and water
115g/4oz plain flour
pinch of salt
chopped fresh parsley and thyme
oil for cooking

FOR THE SAUSAGE CAKES:
1 shallot, finely chopped
15g/¹/₂oz butter
225g/8oz sausagemeat
salt and freshly ground black pepper
dash of Worcestershire sauce
dash of Tabasco
¹/₂ teaspoon grain mustard
25ml/1 fl oz oil

FOR THE GRAVY:
2 onions, chopped
¹/₂ glass white wine
¹/₄ glass Madeira
300ml/¹/₂ pint chicken stock

1 Mix the beaten eggs with the water/milk, and stir in the flour and salt. Beat well until the batter is smooth. Add the herbs.
2 Make the sausage cakes. Sauté the shallot in the butter until soft and translucent and leave to cool.
3 Mix the shallot with the sausagemeat and season with salt and pepper, Worcestershire sauce, Tabasco and mustard. Shape the mixture into 12 small patties.
4 Shallow-fry the patties in a little oil until golden, but do not overcook. Remove from the pan and keep warm.
5 Make the gravy. Sauté the onions in the remaining oil until golden. Strain off any excess fat and add the wine and Madeira. Bring to the boil and cook over high heat to reduce the sauce to almost nothing. Add the stock and cook gently. Check the seasoning.
6 Put a little oil into some Yorkshire pudding moulds and place in a preheated oven at 200°C, 400°F, Gas Mark 6.

7 Remove from the oven and carefully pour in the pudding batter to fill each mould. Place in the oven, and after 5 minutes reduce the heat to 160°C, 325°F, Gas Mark 3 and cook for a further 15-20 minutes.
8 After 10 minutes, when the puddings are set, drop a sausagemeat patty into each one and then replace in the oven until cooked and well risen. Serve with onion gravy.
SERVES: 4

CHICKEN PIE

450g/1lb small pickling onions
50g/2oz butter
25g/1oz flour
600ml/1 pint chicken stock
4 cooked chicken breasts, skinned, boned and chopped
bunch of parsley, finely chopped
24 button mushrooms, quartered
150ml/¹/₄ pint single cream
salt and pepper
225g/8oz shortcrust pastry
1 egg, beaten, for glazing

1 In a little water, slowly cook the small pickling onions until tender. Drain, reserving the cooking liquor.
2 Melt 25g/1oz of the butter, add the flour and stir well. Cook for 2 minutes and then gradually add the reserved onion water and chicken stock, stirring all the time. Bring to the boil, then reduce the heat and simmer for 4 minutes.
3 Add the chicken and parsley to the sauce. Heat the remaining butter and stir in the mushrooms. Toss in the butter and add to the sauce with the cream. Bring to the boil and season to taste. Pour into a pie dish and leave to cool.
4 Roll out the pastry, 3mm/¹/₈ in thick. Use to cover the pie dish, trimming and sealing the edges. Brush with beaten egg and decorate with the pastry trimmings.
5 Bake in a preheated oven at 200°C, 400°F, Gas Mark 6, for 40 minutes. Serve with carrots or broccoli.
SERVES: 4-6

Opposite: Sausage Cakes and Herby Toad

SMOKED BACON AND CABBAGE

1 x 900g/2lb 'meaty' bacon joint
2 onions, peeled and halved
6 cloves
1 bay leaf
50g/2oz butter
225g/8oz carrots, grated
675g/1¹/₂lb cabbage, thinly sliced
salt and freshly ground black pepper

1 Remove the rind from the bacon and place the joint in a large saucepan of cold water with the onions, cloves and bay leaf.
2 Bring to the boil, and then simmer for 1¹/₂ hours. Remove the bacon, pat dry and place in a roasting pan in a preheated oven at 200°C, 400°F, Gas Mark 6, for 20 minutes.
3 Melt the butter in a saucepan and add the grated carrots. Cook gently over low heat for a few minutes and then add the cabbage. Season with salt and freshly ground black pepper, cover with a lid and leave to stew for 5-7 minutes.
4 Arrange the carrots and cabbage on a serving dish. Carve the bacon into slices and lay on top. Serve with stock gravy and potatoes.
SERVES: 4-6

SUET PUDDINGS

If you don't like steak and kidney, you can substitute other traditional fillings. Try a West Country filling of diced pork, apple and sage, or chicken with mushrooms and herbs. Vegetarians can enjoy a delicious root vegetable filling, using parsnips, celeriac and carrots, or even wild mushrooms.

STEAK AND KIDNEY PUDDING

225g/8oz self-raising flour
pinch of salt
115g/4oz shredded suet
150ml/¹/₄ pint cold water
175g/6oz ox kidney
350g/12oz stewing steak
175g/6oz button mushrooms, sliced
1 onion, chopped
small bunch of fresh parsley, thyme and rosemary, chopped
1 tablespoon sunflower oil
¹/₄ glass beef stock
¹/₄ glass red wine
dash of Worcestershire sauce
freshly ground black pepper

1 Mix the flour and salt in a mixing bowl and rub in the suet. Add the cold water slowly, stirring well to form a soft dough, and leave to rest.
2 Grease a large pudding bowl. Roll out two-thirds of the pastry in a circle, and use to line the bowl, leaving some pastry hanging out over the top of the bowl. Roll out the remaining pastry to make a lid.
3 Cut the steak and kidney into1-cm/¹/₂-in dice, and mix with the mushrooms, onion and herbs.
4 Heat the oil in a pan and fry the steak and kidney mixture until lightly coloured. Leave to cool.
5 Put into the pastry lined bowl, and then add a little stock, wine and Worcestershire sauce. Season with salt and pepper. Dampen the pastry edges and cover with the lid. Seal the edges and cut a hole in the centre.
6 Brush with water and place some greaseproof paper on top. Cover with further greaseproof paper and tie securely with string.
7 Place the pudding bowl in the top of a steamer or stand in a large saucepan with water halfway up its sides and cook over low heat for approximately 3 hours.
SERVES: 6

GLAZED GAMMON WITH CIDER

1 x 900g/2lb gammon joint
2 onions, peeled
1 leek
1 celery stick
40 cloves
few sprigs of parsley
sprig of thyme
2 bay leaves
115g/4oz brown sugar
115g/4oz Dijon mustard
300ml/1/2 pint dry cider

1 Soak the gammon in cold water for approximately 12-24 hours. Drain away the soaking liquid and place in a pan of cold water. Bring to the boil, skimming off the scum on the top.
2 Taste the cooking liquid; if it is very salty, change the water and start again. When the water boils, add the onions, leek, celery stick, 12 of the cloves, the parsley, bay leaves and thyme.
3 Simmer slowly for about 1½ hours. To test whether the gammon is cooked, insert the point of a sharp knife and lift up the skin — if cooked, the joint will slide off easily. Remove from the cooking liquor and, with a sharp knife, cut off the skin, discarding any excess fat.
4 Score the fat, not too deeply, in diamond shapes. Mix the brown sugar with enough mustard to make a paste and brush the fat with this mixture. Use more brown sugar, if necessary, and stud the skin with the remaining cloves.
5 Put the gammon in a roasting pan and bake in a preheated oven at 220°C, 425°F, Gas Mark 7. When the sugar has set, after about 5 minutes, mix the rest of the mustard with the cider and use to baste the gammon. When coloured, after about 20-30 minutes, remove the gammon from the oven and leave to rest before carving.
SERVES: 6

BEEF IN BEER

50g/2oz butter
1-2 tablespoons olive oil
2 large onions, roughly chopped
1-2 garlic cloves, crushed
675g/1½lb braising or stewing steak, cubed
2 tablespoons tomato ketchup
1 bay leaf
1 tablespoon soft brown sugar
1 tablespoon red wine vinegar
1½ teaspoons French mustard
4 carrots, cut into batons
300ml/½ pint beef stock
300ml/½ pint brown ale

1 Melt the butter and oil in the pan. Add the onions and garlic and cook until softened, but not browned.
2 Add the beef and stir well until the meat changes colour. Stir in the tomato ketchup, bay leaf, soft brown sugar, red wine vinegar and mustard. Stir well, then add the carrots.
3 Finally, add the stock and the beer, cover the pan and simmer very gently for 2 hours. Alternatively, place in a preheated oven at 180°C, 350°F, Gas Mark 4, for about the same length of time.
4 Serve with broccoli and mashed potatoes for a hearty winter meal.
SERVES: 4

WINTER CASSEROLES

There is nothing so warming and comforting on a cold winter's day as a robust stew or casserole. Use cuts of meat that require slow cooking, such as skirt, chuck steak and stewing steak, or use seasonal venison and game. For a special and distinctive flavour, mix the stock with red or white wine, Madeira, cider or ale.

ROAST PHEASANT WITH CHESTNUTS AND SPROUTS

2 x 675g/1¹/₂lb pheasants
75ml/3 fl oz oil
salt and pepper
450g/1lb potatoes, peeled
50g/2oz butter
450g/1lb prepared Brussels sprouts
225g/8oz shelled chestnuts, roughly chopped
small bunch of chives, snipped

1 Trim the pheasants, leaving the wish bone intact. Heat 25ml/1fl oz of the oil in a roasting pan. Lay the seasoned pheasants on one side in the oil and colour lightly. Turn over and colour the other side.
2 Lay the pheasants on their back and roast in a preheated oven at 200°C, 400°F, Gas Mark 6 for approximately 30 minutes, until cooked and the juices run clear.
3 Meanwhile, cut the potatoes into 5-mm/¹/₄-in dice. Roast them in 25ml/1fl oz of the oil and 25g/1oz of the butter in the oven, alongside the meat, for approximately 15-20 minutes.
4 Plunge the sprouts into boiling salted water and cook until just tender. Drain and refresh in cold water.
5 Heat the remaining oil and butter in a pan and put in the sprouts to reheat them. Mix in the chopped chestnuts and season with salt and pepper.

TRIMMINGS

Pheasants are served traditionally with browned crumbs, bread sauce and game chips. To make the game chips, peel some potatoes and slice very thinly on a mandolin for a lattice effect. Pat dry and then deep fry until crisp and golden brown. Drain and sprinkle with salt.

---

6 Carve the breasts off the pheasants and separate the legs. Arrange the sprouts and chestnuts on 4 serving plates and place a trimmed leg and one breast on top of the sprout mixture. Sprinkle the roast potatoes round the meat. Season and sprinkle with chives.
SERVES: 4

◆

HEN ON HER NEST

1 x 1.8kg/4lb boiling chicken
2 carrots, sliced
2 onions, sliced
1 teaspoon ground ginger
1 teaspoon black peppercorns
pinch of mixed dried herbs
75g/3oz butter
50g/2oz flour
150ml/¹/₄ pint chicken stock or milk
150ml/¹/₄ pint double cream
350g/12oz long-grain rice, boiled
4-6 eggs, hard-boiled and shelled
salt and pepper

1 Place the chicken in a large saucepan with the carrots, onions, spices and herbs. Add enough water to cover the chicken and a good pinch of salt. Bring to the boil, then cover the pan and simmer for 2¹/₂ hours.
2 Transfer the chicken to a baking pan, spread 25g/1oz of the butter over its skin and put in a preheated oven at 200°C, 400°F, Gas Mark 6 for 10 minutes to brown.
3 Meanwhile, melt the remaining butter and stir in the flour to make a roux. Gradually add the chicken stock or milk, stirring over a low heat. Stir in the cream and season to taste.
4 Arrange the cooked rice on a serving platter. Place the chicken in the centre and tuck the shelled eggs underneath. Pour a little of the sauce over the chicken and serve the rest separately.
SERVES: 4-6

Opposite: Roast Pheasant with Chestnuts and Sprouts

VENISON STEAKS WITH STILTON

4 x 225g/8oz venison steaks
50g/2oz butter
115g/4oz Stilton cheese, crumbled
150ml/¹/₄ pint double cream
salt and pepper

1 Sauté the venison steaks quickly in hot butter until nicely browned but still pink inside. Rest as required.
2 Meanwhile, beat together the Stilton and cream and stir into the pan, scraping up all the brown residue and pan juices. Gently warm through, season to taste, and serve with the venison steaks.
SERVES: 4

BUBBLE AND SQUEAK

675g/1¹/₂lb large potatoes
50g/2oz white cabbage, shredded
115g/4oz green cabbage, shredded
25g/1oz chopped onion
2 tablespoons oil
salt and freshly ground black pepper
25g/1oz butter

1 Boil the potatoes in their jackets until half-cooked. Drain and set aside to cool. Blanch the shredded cabbage, then drain and cool.
2 Peel and grate the potatoes and mix with the cabbage. Soften the onion in the oil without colouring and add to the potato and cabbage mixture. Season with salt and pepper and mix together.
3 Melt the butter in a frying pan and add the potato mixture. Stir regularly and then leave over gentle heat to set.
4 Finish in a preheated oven at 200°C, 400°F, Gas Mark 6 for 20 minutes. Turn out and serve.
SERVES: 4-6

NORFOLK STEW AND DUMPLINGS

1 x 1.5kg/3lb chicken, jointed
25g/1oz butter
25g/1oz plain flour
300ml/¹/₂ pint beer
1 chicken stock cube, crumbled
1 onion, chopped
1 carrot, chopped
115g/4oz mushrooms, sliced
2 dessert apples, peeled, cored and chopped
2 teaspoons mixed dried herbs
salt and pepper

FOR THE DUMPLINGS:
175g/6oz self-raising flour
75g/3oz shredded suet
1 teaspoon mixed dried herbs
salt and pepper
cold water, to mix

1 Fry the chicken joints in the butter until browned on both sides. Transfer them to a large flameproof casserole dish.
2 Stir the flour into the remaining butter in the pan and pour in the beer. Add the crumbled stock cube, and stir well over low heat for 2-3 minutes, until the sauce thickens slightly.
3 Pour the sauce over the chicken and add the onion, carrot, mushrooms, apples, herbs and seasoning. Cover and simmer for 1 hour.
4 Mix all the dry dumpling ingredients with cold water to mix to a soft dough. Divide into walnut-sized spoonfuls and drop them into the casserole for the last 20 minutes. Keep the casserole covered so that the dumplings rise.
SERVES: 4

Opposite: Norfolk Stew and Dumplings

PAUL HEATHCOTE

Paul Heathcote trained at the famous Sharrow Bay Hotel, Ullswater, and the Connaught before graduating from Raymond Blanc's renowned Le Manoir aux Quat' Saisons. He now runs his own restaurant and brasserie in Longridge, Preston. In 1994 he was nominated Chef of the Year by the Egon Ronay Guide, and Michelin awarded his restaurant a second star.

LANCASHIRE HOTPOT

2 lamb shanks (approximately 400g/14oz)
3 tablespoons oil
1 onion, chopped
1 carrot, chopped
2 celery sticks, chopped
3 garlic cloves, crushed
4 tomatoes, skinned and seeded
2 bay leaves
sprig of thyme
sprig of rosemary
12 peppercorns
1 teaspoon tomato purée
1.8 litres/3 pints lamb or chicken stock
salt and pepper

FOR THE POTATOES:
115g/4oz melted butter
450g/1lb potatoes, thinly sliced
1/2 onion, thinly sliced
1 carrot, thinly sliced
1 sprig rosemary, chopped
salt and ground white pepper

FOR THE GARNISH:
2 parsnips, cut into 1-cm/1/2-in sticks
2 carrots, cut into 1-cm/1/2-in sticks
2 celery sticks, cut into 1-cm/1/2-in sticks
1 Savoy cabbage, shredded

1 Place the lamb shanks in a large flameproof casserole dish, and fry in the oil until the skin is brown.
2 Add the onion, carrot, celery, garlic and tomatoes, and continue cooking for about 5 minutes, until softened. Add the herbs, peppercorns and tomato purée, and pour in the stock.
3 Cover the casserole and cook in a preheated oven at 180°C, 350°F, Gas Mark 4, for approximately 2 hours.
4 Remove the lamb shanks and keep warm. Sieve the remaining liquid and reduce by boiling until thickened. Season to taste.
5 Meanwhile, brush a 20-cm (8-in) square ovenproof dish with some of the melted butter and sprinkle with salt and pepper.
6 Salt the potatoes to avoid curling at the ends. Mix them with the onion and carrot and the melted butter. Season with salt, pepper and rosemary.
7 Arrange a layer of potatoes in the base of the dish and around the sides, overlapping well. Place the remaining vegetables in the dish, cover with a lid or foil and bake in the preheated oven for about 45 minutes, until cooked and golden brown. Cool for 30 minutes before turning out.
8 Boil the vegetables for the garnish in lightly salted water until just tender: 10-15 minutes for the parsnips, carrots and celery; 3-5 minutes for the cabbage.
9 Reheat the potatoes and serve with the lamb on individual serving plates. Serve with the sauce and the vegetable garnish.
SERVES: 4

IRISH STEW

900g/2lb middle neck lamb chops, trimmed of excess fat
1.5kg/3lb potatoes, sliced
450g/1lb onions, sliced
115g/4oz sliced leek
115g/4oz sliced celery
600ml/1 pint lamb or chicken stock
small bunch of mixed fresh herbs
225g/8oz Savoy cabbage, outer leaves removed
15g/¹/₂oz butter
salt and freshly ground black pepper
2 tablespoons chopped fresh parsley
few celery leaves, chopped

1 Put the chops in a saucepan with the potatoes, onions, leek and celery. Add the stock and herbs.
2 Cover the pan with a lid and place over low heat. Simmer gently for 1¹/₂ to 2 hours, until the lamb is cooked thoroughly.
3 Plunge the less green cabbage leaves into boiling salted water and then refresh. Arrange on a clean tea-towel and set aside.
4 Chop the inside leaves finely and sweat gently in the butter. Season to taste with salt and black pepper.
5 Put a tablespoon of the cooked cabbage on top of each leaf and, using the tea-towel, squeeze the cabbage leaf into a small ball shape. Place in an ovenproof dish and set aside.
6 Take the lamb out of the liquor and keep warm. Spoon the cooked potato mixture out of the liquor in the pan into a food processor or blender and blend until smooth and creamy. Season to taste.
7 Pour some of the liquor over the cabbage balls and reheat in the oven.
8 Arrange the chops in the middle of a serving dish and pour the sauce over them. Decorate with the potato pureé and arrange the cabbage balls around the edge of the dish. Serve sprinkled with chopped parsley and celery leaves.
SERVES: 4

Below: Paul Heathcote's Lancashire Hotpot

CHAPTER TWO

SNACKS & FAST FOOD

The recipes in this section are ideal for the busy person who has little time for cooking but enjoys good food. There is a selection of mouthwatering snacks and more substantial dishes which can all be whisked up in a hurry and then eaten at leisure. This fast food is delicious and nutritious and takes less time to cook than many convenience packaged foods.

Frittata (see page 27)

FILO SAMOSAS

2 tablespoons vegetable oil
1 medium onion, finely chopped
115g/4oz peas, fresh or frozen
1/2 tablespoon finely grated, peeled fresh ginger
1/2-1 fresh green chilli, seeded and finely chopped
2 tablespoons finely chopped fresh coriander
2 tablespoons water
450g/1lb boiled potatoes, cut into small dice
1 teaspoon salt, or to taste
1 level teaspoon ground coriander seeds
1 level teaspoon ground cumin seeds
1/4 teaspoon cayenne pepper
1-2 tablespoons lemon juice
1 packet fresh or defrosted filo pastry
50-75g/2-3oz melted butter

1 To make the filling, heat the oil in a large frying pan over medium heat, until hot. Add the onions, and stir-fry until they begin to brown at the edges. Stir in the peas, ginger, chilli, fresh coriander and the water. Cover the pan, lower the heat and simmer until the peas are cooked, adding a little more water if the mixture seems to dry out.

2 Add the potatoes, salt, coriander and cumin seeds, cayenne and lemon juice. Cook for a further 3-4 minutes over low heat, mixing well.

3 Check the flavour and add more salt or lemon juice to taste, if necessary. Remove from the heat and allow to cool.

4 Take one sheet of the filo pastry and brush with melted butter. Keep the rest of the pastry covered with a damp cloth. Place another sheet of pastry on top and brush this with butter.

5 Cut the pastry into strips, about 5 or 7.5 cm/2 or 3 in wide, depending on the size of the sheets, but you should have 5 strips per double sheet. Place a heaped teaspoon of stuffing at the top of each strip and fold into triangles. Continue with the remaining sheets of pastry.

6 Place on a baking tray, brush with the remaining melted butter and place in a preheated oven at 200°C, 400°F, Gas Mark 6, for approximately 15 minutes, or until the samosas are golden brown.
SERVES: 4

TORTILLA (SPANISH OMELETTE)

2 tablespoons olive oil
675g/1 1/2lb small waxy potatoes, scrubbed and diced
bunch of spring onions, trimmed and chopped
6 eggs
salt and freshly ground black pepper, to taste

1 Heat the oil in a very large frying pan, and gently sauté the potatoes for 5 minutes, turning them frequently. Add the spring onions and mix well with the potatoes.

2 Beat the eggs in a bowl with the salt and pepper. Pour over the potatoes and cook over very gentle heat for about 5 minutes, by which time the potatoes should be cooked and the eggs set at the sides and base of the omelette.

3 Finish off the omelette by browning the top under a preheated hot grill. Serve warm cut into wedges with a green salad.
SERVES: 4

CROQUE MONSIEUR

8 slices thickly sliced white bread
8 slices cheese
4 slices ham
2 eggs, beaten
oil for shallow frying

1 Make sandwiches, using a layer of bread, a slice of cheese, a slice of ham, another slice of cheese and a slice of bread on top. Press down firmly and cut in half diagonally.

2 Dip each bread triangle into beaten egg and then fry in hot oil for a minute or two on each side until browned and crisp.
SERVES: 4

FRED'S CHEESY FRENCH TOAST

2 eggs
4 tablespoons milk
8 slices white bread
4 slices Cheddar cheese
salt and pepper
oil for shallow frying

1 Beat the eggs with the milk, and season with salt and pepper.
2 Place a slice of cheese between 2 slices of bread and cut in half, or in quarters if preferred. Repeat with the remaining bread and cheese.
3 Soak both sides of each sandwich in the beaten egg and milk mixture.
4 Fry the sandwiches in a little hot oil until golden brown on both sides, and the cheese filling has melted. Serve with a green salad.
SERVES: 4

FRITTATA

2 onions, finely chopped
3 tablespoons olive oil
2 red peppers, seeded and sliced
4 courgettes, sliced
few sprigs of fresh marjoram and thyme, chopped
salt and freshly ground black pepper
6 eggs
50g/2oz grated Parmesan cheese
15g/¹/₂oz butter

1 Sauté the onions gently in the olive oil until soft and translucent. Stir in the red peppers and courgettes and continue cooking until cooked and golden. Add the herbs and seasoning.
2 Beat the eggs in a large bowl and stir in the sautéed vegetables and the Parmesan cheese.

3 Heat the butter in a frying pan and pour in the egg mixture. Cook over gentle heat until the omelette is set and golden brown underneath. Pop it under a preheated hot grill to set it and brown the top. Serve lukewarm, cut into wedges, with a fresh salad.
SERVES: 4

POACHED EGGS ON HAM AND SPINACH

dash of malt vinegar
good pinch of salt
4 eggs
450g/1lb spinach, washed and trimmed
25g/1oz butter
4 slices ham
300ml/¹/₂ pint white sauce (see page 71)
50g/2oz grated cheese
50ml/2fl oz whipped cream
pinch of paprika
50g/2oz white breadcrumbs
salt and pepper

1 Bring a saucepan of water up to the boil and add a dash of vinegar and some salt. Poach the eggs and then plunge them into iced water when cooked. Take them out quickly and dry them with absorbent kitchen paper.
2 Cook the spinach gently in the butter, season to taste and divide between 4 dishes.
3 Warm the slices of ham and arrange them on top of the spinach. Put the eggs on top of the ham and season to taste with salt and pepper.
4 Heat the white sauce and stir in the cheese, whipped cream and paprika. Pour over the top of the eggs.
5 Sprinkle with breadcrumbs, then place under a preheated grill until golden brown and serve.
SERVES: 4

Will Carling is the best-known rugby player in the UK today. England's youngest captain for 57 years, he is also his country's most-capped centre and holder of the world record for most international wins as captain. Outside of rugby and running his own management company, Will enjoys cooking for his friends and family.

CARLING'S STIR-FRY

You could use pieces of chicken in this recipe but for a vegetarian dish I used quorn pieces or tofu. Quorn is a myco-protein which is grown in big tanks – it is a relation of the mushroom. Because it is bound into pieces with egg albumen, not all vegetarians want to eat it. Tofu is made from the fermented curd of soya beans, and is suitable for vegetarians and vegans. Take care when cooking with it that you handle it gently, as the pieces can easily break up.

175g/6oz quorn pieces
2 tablespoons oyster sauce
1 tablespoon soy sauce
1 tablespoon sherry
2 tablespoons sesame oil
1-cm/^{1}/2-in piece fresh root ginger, peeled and diced
1 carrot, cut into thin batons
2 spring onions, chopped
115g/4oz broccoli florets
115g/4oz beansprouts
^{1}/2 red pepper, seeded and sliced
^{1}/2 yellow pepper, seeded and sliced
115g/4oz button mushrooms, sliced
1 tablespoon cornflour
4 tablespoons stock
salt and pepper
boiled rice, to serve

1 Marinate the quorn pieces in the oyster and soy sauces and sherry for 20 minutes.
2 Heat the oil in a wok and, when hot, add the ginger. Stir-fry for 1 minute, then add the carrot and spring onions. Continue stir-frying for 1 minute.
3 Add the quorn pieces together with the sauce from the marinade. After 30 seconds, add the broccoli, beansprouts, peppers and mushrooms, and stir-fry briskly until just heated through but still crisp.
4 Blend the cornflour with the stock to make a smooth mixture, and stir into the wok. Keep stirring until thickened. Serve immediately with boiled rice.
SERVES: 2

Opposite: Carling's Stir-fry

PASTA WITH PESTO

450g/1lb spaghetti, tagliatelle or fettucine

FOR THE PESTO SAUCE:
*30 basil leaves
2 garlic cloves, peeled
handful of pine kernels, toasted
1/2 tablespoon grated Parmesan cheese
115ml/4fl oz olive oil*

1 Bring a large saucepan of salted water to the boil, and add 1 tablespoon of oil. Slowly add the dried pasta (if using) or plunge in the fresh pasta. Cook until *al dente* (tender to the bite) – about 10 minutes for dried pasta, 4 minutes for fresh pasta.
2 Drain the pasta in a colander and refresh under hot running water. Drain and transfer to a large bowl.
3 Meanwhile, make the pesto sauce. Pound the basil leaves (wiped not washed) with the garlic and pine kernels to form a paste. Gradually add the cheese and then blend in the olive oil with a wooden spoon.
4 Sprinkle the pesto sauce over the top. Stir the sauce through the pasta, using two forks, and serve immediately.
SERVES: 4

PENNE WITH CHILLI SAUCE

*4 tablespoons olive oil
2 garlic cloves, peeled and crushed
2 chilli peppers, seeded and finely chopped
1 x 400g/14oz can chopped tomatoes or 1 x 450g/1lb
carton or bottled passata
salt and pepper
375g/13oz dried penne
2 tablespoons finely chopped fresh parsley
75g/3oz freshly grated Parmesan cheese*

1 Heat the oil and briefly fry the garlic and the chilli. Add

the tomatoes and cook for 5 minutes. Season to taste with salt and pepper.
2 Cook the penne in a large saucepan of boiling lightly salted water until tender, about 5-6 minutes, and then drain.
3 Stir the cooked pasta and the parsley into the sauce and mix together with the Parmesan cheese. Serve immediately.
SERVES: 4

CHINESE NUTS AND NOODLES

*1 layer egg noodles (half a 250g/9oz packet)
1 1/2 tablespoons oil
1 cm/1/2 in fresh root ginger, peeled and crushed
1 garlic clove, crushed
1/2 bunch spring onions, sliced
50g/2oz mange-tout
2 large open-cap mushrooms, sliced
75g/3oz cashew nuts*

FOR THE SAUCE:
*1 tablespoon soy sauce
3 tablespoons water
2 teaspoons cornflour
1 tablespoon sherry or rice vinegar*

1 Cook the noodles according to the instructions on the packet. While they are cooking, heat the oil in a wok and stir-fry the ginger and garlic for 1 minute. Add the spring onions and stir-fry for 30 seconds, then add the mange-tout and mushrooms. Stir-fry for a few seconds and then add the cashew nuts. Heat through gently.
2 In a small bowl, mix the soy sauce and water with the cornflour. Pour the sherry into the stir-fried mixture and then stir in the cornflour mixture. Stir until thickened.
3 Drain the cooked noodles and mix with the nutty sauce. Serve immediately.
SERVES: 2

Opposite: Penne with Chilli Sauce

PIZZA

FOR THE DOUGH:
115ml/4fl oz warm water
1/2 teaspoon sugar
1 1/2 teaspoons dried yeast
1/2 teaspoon salt
225g/8oz strong plain flour
1 egg, beaten
1 teaspoon vegetable oil

FOR THE TOMATO SAUCE:
1 tablespoon oil
1 onion, finely chopped
2 garlic cloves, crushed
1 x 400g/14oz can tomatoes
1 teaspoon dried mixed herbs
*1 tablespoon sun-dried tomato
purée*
salt and pepper

FOR THE TOPPING:
50g/2oz mushrooms, thinly sliced
*115g/4oz mozzarella cheese, thinly
sliced*
1 tablespoon olive oil
10 black olives, stoned
fresh basil leaves, to garnish

1 Mix the warm water with the sugar in a small bowl. When dissolved, sprinkle in the yeast. Stir and leave for 10 minutes until frothy. In a large bowl, mix together the salt and flour, make a well in the middle and pour in the yeast mixture. Mix to a soft dough that leaves the sides of the bowl clean.

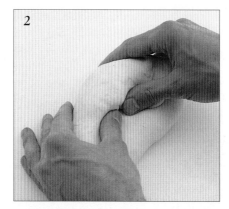

2 Knead the dough on a lightly floured surface for 10 minutes. Place in a well-oiled bowl, cover with a cloth and leave in a warm place until doubled in size. Knock down the dough and knead for 5 minutes. Press out with your hands to a thin round or rectangle on a greased baking sheet.

3 Make the tomato sauce. Heat the oil and fry the onion and garlic until soft. Add the tomatoes, herbs and tomato paste and simmer for 10 minutes, until thickened. Purée in a blender or food processor, and season to taste.

4 Spread the tomato sauce over the pizza base, and scatter the mushrooms and cheese over the top. Sprinkle with olive oil and olives, and bake in a preheated oven at 220°C, 425°F, Gas Mark 7 for 20 minutes. Serve garnished with torn basil leaves.
SERVES: 3-4

BRUSCHETTA

This quick bread, garlic and olive oil snack is often eaten by the olive pickers as a way of tasting the new oil.

4 tablespoons good-quality olive oil
4 garlic cloves, chopped
8 slices French bread

1 Warm the olive oil in a pan with the chopped garlic. Brush this over both sides of the slices of French bread.
2 Toast in a preheated oven at 200°C, 400°F, Gas mark 6 for about 10 minutes, until golden brown.
3 Serve the bruschetta as an accompaniment to a main dish, or as a snack or starter, by topping each slice of bread with a slice of grilled red pepper, and a little cottage or goat's cheese.
SERVES: 3-4

CROSTINI

25g/1oz butter
25ml/1fl oz olive oil
1/2 onion, chopped
4 fresh sage leaves
225g/8oz chicken livers, trimmed
splash of Cognac
juice of 1/2 lemon
1/2 loaf white bread, sliced
1 garlic clove, crushed
150ml/1/4 pint olive oil
salt and freshly ground black pepper

1 Heat half of the butter and half of the oil in a frying pan. Add the onion and sage, and cook slowly for 5 minutes.
2 Heat the remaining butter and oil in another pan and gently sauté the chicken livers. Add the Cognac and cook gently for 1 minute.
3 Using a slotted spoon, put half of the livers and half of the onion and sage mixture into a food processor. Roughly chop, season with salt and pepper and transfer to a bowl.
4 Chop the rest of the livers on a board to keep them in fairly large pieces. Mix them with the processed mixture and the remaining onion and sage. Check the seasoning and mix in the lemon juice.
5 Toast the bread and, using a round cutter, cut into small rounds, approximately 5cm/2in across. Mix the garlic with the olive oil and quickly dip the toasted bread into the oil. Spread some chicken liver mixture on each slice.
SERVES: 4

Opposite: Crostini and Bruschetta

TOAST TOPPING IDEAS

For a quick snack, you can top some toasted bread with one of the following:

1 Slices of tomato and blue cheese, e.g. Dolcelatte. Pop under a hot grill until melted.

2 Mashed up avocado with a little salt, pepper and crushed garlic or garlic purée. Dust with paprika and grill, if wished.

3 Spread one side of the toast thinly with French mustard, then top with a small can of creamed mushrooms. Mix in some chopped boiled ham and pop under a hot grill to heat through.

4 Drain a small can of tuna and flake with a fork. Mix with 1 dessertspoon of mayonnaise and some chopped parsley or chives. Brown under a hot grill.

5 Sprinkle hot buttered toast with a little cinnamon and sugar for a traditional teatime treat on a cold winter's day.

6 Place a slice of smoked salmon on some hot buttered toast, top with a slice of cheese and pop under a hot grill.

CHAMPANY BEEFBURGERS

This recipe is reproduced by kind permission of C. R. Davison, Champany Inn, West Lothian

1.5kg/3lb lean shoulder steak
1 egg
25g/1oz dry butcher's rusk (mixed with sufficient water to swell)
pinch of salt
small pinch of black pepper
25g/1oz back bacon fat

Mince the steak and mix with the remaining ingredients. Shape into patties, and then grill or fry them on both sides.
SERVES: 10-12

SALMON PATTIE CAKES

115g/4oz button mushrooms, diced
40g/1¹/₂oz butter
squeeze of lemon juice
15g/¹/₂oz flour
150ml/¹/₄ pint milk
1 egg yolk
pinch of ground nutmeg
225g/8oz cooked salmon, skinned, boned and flaked
1 egg, beaten
50g/2oz breadcrumbs, toasted
salt and pepper
oil for shallow frying
lemon wedges, to serve

1 Toss the mushrooms in 15g/¹/₂oz of the butter, until cooked and golden brown. Squeeze the lemon juice over the mushrooms and put aside.
2 Melt the remaining butter in a saucepan, stir in the flour and cook gently without colouring. Add the milk gradually, stirring all the time to make a thick sauce. Remove from the heat and beat in the egg yolk.

3 Add the mushrooms and their juices, and return to the heat. Stir over low heat until thickened. Season with salt, pepper and nutmeg, and stir in the salmon.
4 Heat through gently and then transfer to a bowl and refrigerate; leave to solidify.
5 With well-floured hands, mould the salmon mixture into 6 equal-sized balls, or 8 equal-sized smaller ones. Press down into patties, dip into beaten egg and then coat with toasted breadcrumbs.
7 Fry the patties in hot oil, until golden brown, and serve with lemon wedges.
SERVES: 4

SPICY NUT BURGERS

25g/1oz butter
1 onion, finely diced
1 tablespoon chopped fresh parsley
15g/¹/₂oz wholemeal flour
150ml/¹/₄ pint milk
225g/8oz chopped mixed nuts
1 tablespoon soy sauce
1 tablespoon tomato purée
175g/6oz wholemeal breadcrumbs
1 egg, beaten
salt and pepper

1 Melt the butter in a saucepan and add the onion. Fry gently until soft and translucent. Add the parsley and stir in the flour. Cook for 2 minutes, then gradually add the milk, stirring. Bring to the boil and boil until thickened. Simmer gently for 1-2 minutes.
2 Add the nuts, soy sauce, tomato purée, breadcrumbs and seasoning and mix well. If the mixture is too stiff, add some beaten egg.
3 Divide into 8 pieces and shape into burgers. The mixture is sticky so you will need to flour your hands to shape them.
4 Grill the burgers for 4 minutes on each side. Serve them with a spicy salsa.
SERVES: 4

TOFU BURGERS

225g/8oz tofu
115g/4oz carrot, finely grated
115g/4oz wholemeal breadcrumbs
1 small onion, finely chopped
1 teaspoon piri piri seasoning, or chilli powder
1 tablespoon Worcestershire sauce
2 teaspoons yeast extract
1 egg, beaten
salt and pepper

1 Drain and mash the tofu. Add the carrot, breadcrumbs, onion, piri piri seasoning or chilli powder, Worcestershire sauce, yeast extract and enough beaten egg to bind to a firm texture. Season with salt and pepper and mix well.
2 Divide the mixture into 8 pieces and shape into burgers. Chill in the refrigerator for 30 minutes.
3 Grill or barbecue the burgers for about 4 minutes on each side.
SERVES: 4

BEEFBURGERS

If you make your own, you know what's in them, and they can be better value for money than buying ready-made burgers. You can either make 4 'quarter-pounders', or 8 smaller (50g/2oz) burgers.

450g/1lb minced beef
salt and pepper
1 small onion, chopped (optional)
breadcrumbs, for mixing (optional)
1 egg, beaten (optional)

1 Mix the minced beef with the salt and pepper in a mixing bowl. Shape into balls with your hands, and then flatten into burger shapes. If you like your burgers tasting of onion, add a little finely chopped onion to the mince. If you want the mixture to go further, add some

breadcrumbs. Bind the mixture together with beaten egg.
2 You can fry or grill the burgers: grilling is better to lose some of the fat. Alternatively, fry them in a non-stick pan without adding any fat, or just brush the surface with a little oil before frying or grilling.
SERVES: 4

Note: adding a spoonful of tomato ketchup to the mixture makes a tasty addition.

PORK ALLA ROMANA

675g/1¹/₂lb fillet of pork
8 slices Parma ham
8 sage leaves
flour for dusting
1 teaspoon olive oil
75g/3oz butter
¹/₂ glass Madeira
splash of dry white wine
juice of ¹/₂ lemon
2 tablespoons chopped fresh parsley
salt and freshly ground black pepper

1 Cut the pork fillet into 8 evenly sized pieces. Lay a piece of pork between 2 sheets of cling film and tap out with a rolling pin until flattened. Remove the cling film. Repeat with the other pork pieces.
2 Lay a slice of ham on top of each piece of pork and top with a sage leaf. Secure with a wooden cocktail stick.
3 Sprinkle the pork with flour and shake off any excess. Fry quickly on both sides in the oil and butter until golden brown. Remove and keep warm.
4 Pour off any excess fat from the pan, then add the Madeira and wine and boil to reduce by half. Add the lemon juice and parsley, and check the seasoning. Pour the sauce over the pork.
SERVES: 4

CHAPTER THREE

SUPPER DISHES

◆

Here are some sparkling and versatile recipes for a wide range of supper dishes. They are all relatively easy to cook, and include filling soups that can be served with cheese and crusty bread for a light meal, as well as more substantial pasta and chicken dishes. For hot days when you fancy something light and refreshing, there are sensational salads and sizzling ribs and chops.

Mediterranean Pasta (see page 40)

SCOTCH BROTH

450g/1lb shin of beef
2 litres/3¹/₂ pints cold water
1 teaspoon salt
2 tablespoons pearl barley, washed and drained
2 tablespoons yellow split peas
1 tablespoon whole dried peas, soaked overnight
2 medium-sized carrots, cleaned and diced
2 leeks, trimmed and sliced
3 tablespoons diced swede
1 medium onion, finely chopped
1 good handful finely chopped fresh parsley
salt and pepper, to taste

1 Put the meat, water, salt, washed barley, split peas and soaked peas into a large saucepan. Bring slowly to the boil and skim. Simmer for about 1 hour and then remove the meat from the saucepan. (This can then be served warm as a separate course with vegetables and boiled potatoes.)
2 Add the finely diced vegetables and onion to the saucepan and continue to simmer until the vegetables are tender. Finish the broth by adding the parsley. Season with salt and pepper to taste.
3 Serve hot with oatcakes.
SERVES: 6

MEDITERRANEAN PASTA

450g/1lb spaghetti
5 tablespoons olive oil
2 garlic cloves, crushed
4 anchovy fillets, rinsed and chopped
1 fresh red chilli, seeded and chopped
450g/1lb fresh tomatoes, skinned, seeded and chopped
1 tablespoon capers
115g/4oz black olives, stoned and sliced
2 tablespoons chopped fresh parsley
salt and freshly ground black pepper

1 Cook the spaghetti in plenty of boiling, salted water with a dash of olive oil to prevent it sticking, for about 12-15 minutes. It is cooked when it is *al dente* (tender to the bite). Drain and transfer to a large serving bowl.
2 Meanwhile, heat the olive oil in a frying pan, and add the crushed garlic, and then the anchovies and chilli. Stir-fry for a couple of minutes, then add the tomatoes, capers and olives.
3 Simmer the sauce for 5-10 minutes, until thickened slightly. Stir in the parsley and season to taste.
4 Pour the sauce over the spaghetti, toss together and serve immediately.
SERVES: 4

SUSAN'S KEDGEREE

1 onion, finely chopped
50g/2oz butter
¹/₂ teaspoon curry powder
¹/₂ teaspoon turmeric
225g/8oz long-grain rice
400ml/14fl oz water
1 x 200g/7oz can stoned black olives, drained
2 x 200g/7oz cans tuna, drained and flaked
juice of ¹/₂ lemon
2 tablespoons chopped fresh parsley
4 hard-boiled eggs, shelled and quartered
salt and pepper

1 Fry the onion in the butter until soft. Add the curry powder and turmeric and fry gently for 2-3 minutes.
2 Add the rice and water, and bring up to the boil. Cover the pan and simmer gently for 15 minutes. Stir well and check whether the rice is cooked. If not, you may need to add a little more water and simmer for a few more minutes.
3 Add the olives, tuna, lemon juice (and grated rind if you wish), half of the parsley, and salt and pepper to taste.
4 Heat through gently, and serve garnished with the quartered boiled eggs and the rest of the parsley.
SERVES: 4

Opposite: Smoked Haddock Lasagne

SMOKED HADDOCK LASAGNE

300g/10oz dried lasagne
300ml/¹/₂ pint white sauce
450g/1lb smoked haddock, diced
12 plum tomatoes, skinned, seeded and chopped
1 garlic clove, crushed
1 bunch parsley, chopped
1 tablespoon olive oil
115g/4oz soft Italian cheese, e.g. Taleggio, diced
50g/2oz grated Parmesan cheese
50g/2oz white breadcrumbs
salt and pepper

1 Cook the lasagne in boiling salted water with a couple of drops of olive oil until *al dente* (tender to the bite). Refresh in cold water and drain thoroughly.
2 Place a sheet of lasagne in the base of a well-greased baking sheet and cover with a layer of white sauce.
3 Mix the haddock with the tomato, garlic, parsley and seasoning, and scatter over the white sauce layer. Sprinkle with olive oil and add some diced Italian cheese.
4 Cover with a sheet of pasta on top and continue layering up the dish in this way, alternating the lasagne with the filling and finishing with a layer of white sauce.
5 Sprinkle with Parmesan cheese and breadcrumbs. Bake in a preheated oven at 180°C, 350°F, Gas Mark 4 for 40-45 minutes, until the top is crisp and golden brown. Serve immediately.
SERVES: 4

MURDO MACSWEEN

Murdo MacSween comes from Harris in Scotland and speaks fluent Gaelic. He gained his first Michelin star at Walton's Restaurant in London, and was one of the first five British chefs to cook at Maxim's in Paris. He has participated in Gaelic cookery programmes for Scottish television.

CULLEN SKINK

300g/10oz mixed onion, leek, celery and garlic, chopped
25g/1oz butter
250ml/8fl oz white wine
600ml/1 pint fish stock
300g/10oz smoked haddock fillet
300g/10oz potatoes, peeled and diced
150ml/¼ pint double cream

FOR THE GARNISH:
115g/4oz white of leek, finely chopped
25g/1oz butter
12 peeled prawns
2 tablespoons chopped fresh chives

1 Cook the onion, leek, celery and garlic gently in the butter over low heat, until soft. Add the white wine, increase the heat and reduce by half. Pour in the fish stock and bring to the boil.
2 Reduce the heat and add the smoked haddock fillet. Simmer gently for 10 minutes, then remove the haddock and keep warm. Add the diced potatoes to the soup and simmer for 15-20 minutes.
3 Liquidize the soup in a blender or food processor, and then return to the saucepan. Reheat gently over low heat.
4 Meanwhile, prepare the garnish. Sweat the leek in the butter until soft. Add the prawns and cook for 1 minute. Place the garnish in a soup tureen and pour in the soup. Flake the haddock, discarding any skin and bones, and stir into the soup. Sprinkle with chopped chives and serve.
SERVES: 4-6

SOUPS FOR SUPPER

Cullen Skink is a traditional Scottish dish, which can be served at Hogmanay or on Burns Night. For a more informal supper, have it piping hot with chunks of crusty bread.

Often we feel hungry but don't want to eat a large meal. On these occasions a bowl of soup can make an easy meal. To make soups more sustaining, try adding extra vegetables, beans, lentils, pasta and barley. You can buy special soup mixes to add to vegetable soups to bulk them out and add texture and flavour. Check before using to see if the mixtures require pre-soaking. For an interesting finish, you can try topping soups with grated cheese, plain or garlic croûtons, pieces of crisp-fried bacon, snipped herbs or shredded vegetables.

Opposite: Cullen Skink

ITALIAN MEAT LOAF

2 red peppers
olive oil for roasting
2 courgettes, trimmed and diced
2 garlic cloves, crushed
25g/1oz butter
1 onion, diced
115g/4oz mushrooms, chopped
675g/1¹/₂lb minced beef
25g/1oz Gruyère cheese, grated
3 tablespoons chopped parsley
1 egg, beaten
225g/8oz boiled new potatoes, skinned and diced
salt and freshly ground black pepper

FOR THE MARINATED RED ONIONS:
2 red onions, thinly sliced
12 peppercorns
1 bay leaf
white wine vinegar

1 Make the marinated red onions. Blanch the onions in boiling water, then drain and put in a bowl with the peppercorns and bay leaf. Cover with a mixture of one-third vinegar to two-thirds boiling water, and leave for 1½ hours.
2 Place the red peppers in a pan with some olive oil and roast in a preheated oven at 200°C, 400°F, Gas Mark 6 for 15-20 minutes, until soft. Set aside to cool.
3 When the peppers are cool, remove the skin and seeds, and dice the flesh.
4 Sauté the courgettes and garlic in the butter until softened. Season, remove from the pan and drain.
5 Soften the onion in the butter, then remove and drain. Repeat with the mushrooms.
6 Mix the onions, mince and Gruyère and stir in the parsley. Bind with a beaten egg and season with salt and pepper.
7 Lay a sheet of greaseproof paper on a tea towel and place the minced beef mixture in the centre. Mould into a rectangle, 1cm/¹/₂in thick.
8 Mix the courgettes, potatoes, mushrooms and peppers and sprinkle over the meat, leaving 5mm/¹/₄in clear around the edge. Roll up like a Swiss roll and then place the meat loaf on a well greased baking sheet.
9 Bake in a preheated oven at 200°C, 400°F, Gas Mark 6 for 45 minutes. Leave to set, then cut into slices, sprinkle with the marinated red onions and serve.
SERVES: 6

CHICKEN FAJITAS

2 red peppers, halved and seeded
2 tablespoons olive oil
2 onions, sliced
3 garlic cloves, crushed
2 teaspoons minced chilli
2 large chicken breasts, skinned and boned
2 teaspoons chopped fresh coriander
grated zest of ¹/₂ lime
2 tablespoons lime juice
4 wheat or corn tortillas
4 tablespoons sour cream

FOR THE GARNISH:
tomato salsa, guacamole and lime wedges

1 Place the red peppers, skin-side upwards, under a preheated grill, and cook until well charred. Leave to cool slightly and then peel off the skin. Cut the flesh into thin slices.
2 Heat the olive oil and add the onions, garlic and chilli. Fry gently for a few minutes, until the onion softens.
3 Cut the chicken into narrow strips and add to the pan. Fry for 4-5 minutes until cooked through, stirring occasionally.
4 Add the peppers, coriander, lime zest and juice, and continue cooking for 2-3 minutes. Season to taste.
5 Wrap the tortillas loosely in some aluminium foil and heat in a preheated oven at 180°C, 350°F, Gas Mark 4, for 5 minutes. Remove the tortillas, divide the chicken mixture between them and fold over.
6 Serve the fajitas topped with a spoonful of sour cream, garnished with tomato salsa, guacamole and lime wedges.
SERVES: 4

Opposite: Chicken Fajitas

BACON RATATOUILLE

This makes a good topping for baked jacket potatoes. Alternatively, you can mop up the juices with hunks of bread.

1 tablespoon vegetable oil
1 medium onion, chopped
2 garlic cloves, crushed
225g/8oz diced bacon
2 medium courgettes, sliced
6 tomatoes, skinned and quartered
1 x 230g/8oz can chopped tomatoes
1 tablespoon tomato purée
freshly ground black pepper

1 Heat the oil and sauté the onion and garlic for a few minutes, until softened. Add the bacon and fry until crisp.
2 Add the sliced courgettes, quartered tomatoes, canned tomatoes and tomato purée. Stir well, cover the pan and simmer for 10 minutes.
3 Season with freshly ground black pepper and serve with potatoes or bread.
SERVES: 3-4

MARINADES

Marinades not only add subtle flavours to meat and poultry, but they also tenderize and moisten it before cooking. You can use wine, oil, vinegar, fruit juice, spices, herbs, garlic and onion to marinate lamb, pork, beef, game and chicken.

For a more oriental marinade, add ginger, soy sauce, chillies and honey. Always leave to marinate in a cool place, preferably the refrigerator, for at least 1 hour or overnight.

FINGER LICKIN' CHOPS

You will need a selection of lamb chops, e.g. loin, cutlets, chump, or whatever is available. Choose one of the following marinades to suit your preference:

12 lamb chops
fresh herbs, to garnish, (e.g. mint, oregano, parsley, sage)

FOR THE MINT MARINADE:
3 level tablespoons mint jelly
1 tablespoon wine vinegar
2 tablespoons oil
salt and pepper

FOR THE GINGER MARINADE:
3 level tablespoons ginger preserve
1 tablespoon wine vinegar
2 tablespoons oil
grated rind of 1/2 lemon
1 tablespoon lemon juice
salt and pepper

FOR THE GARLIC AND
CORIANDER MARINADE:
4 garlic cloves, crushed
1 tablespoon chopped fresh coriander
4 tablespoons oil
2 tablespoons red wine
salt and pepper

1 Make up the marinade of your choice and pour over the lamb chops. Leave the chops in the refrigerator or a cold place to marinate for at least 2 hours.
2 The chops can be barbecued, grilled or roasted in a preheated oven at 200°C, 400°F, Gas Mark 6 – the time will depend on their thickness and how rare or well cooked you like your lamb.
3 When cooked, arrange the chops on a platter. Garnish with fresh herbs and spoon a little marinade over the chops before serving. Serve with hash browns.
SERVES: 4

RED HOT RIBS

1.4kg/3lb Chinese-style pork spare ribs
2 garlic cloves, crushed
1-2 fresh green chillies, seeded and finely chopped
1-cm/¹/₂-in piece of root ginger, peeled and finely chopped
3 tablespoons clear honey
3 tablespoons dark soft brown sugar
4 tablespoons tomato ketchup
4 tablespoons dry sherry/wine vinegar
2 tablespoons soya sauce
2 tablespoons Hoisin sauce
2 tablespoons French mustard
4 teaspoons chilli sauce
salt and pepper
spring onion tassles, to garnish

1 Place the spare ribs in a large roasting pan. Put all the remaining ingredients for the marinade in a jug and whisk well. Pour the marinade over the ribs, brushing the sauce over the ribs to coat them.
2 Set aside in a cool place, such as the refrigerator, to marinate for 30 minutes.
3 Bake the ribs uncovered in a preheated oven at 180°C, 350°F, Gas Mark 4 for 30 minutes, then turn the ribs over and bake for a further 30 minutes, until the pork is tender and the sauce is syrupy.
4 Transfer the ribs to a serving dish. Serve with plain boiled rice or a crisp green salad, and garnish with spring onion tassles.
SERVES: 4

Below: Red Hot Ribs

MOROCCAN FLAN

150g/5oz bulgar wheat or cracked
wheat
450g/1lb minced lamb
1 onion, finely chopped
leaves of 4 sprigs of mint
few sprigs of parsley, chopped
2 level teaspoons ground cumin
1 egg
2 garlic cloves, peeled and thinly
sliced
50g/2oz pine nuts
salt and pepper

1 Put the bulgar wheat in a bowl and cover with cold water. The water should be at least 2.5 cm/1 in above the level of the bulgar wheat. Leave to soak for 1 hour, then tip into a bowl and squeeze to drain off any excess water.

2 In a large bowl, mix together the drained bulgar wheat, minced lamb, onion, mint, parsley and cumin with salt and pepper. Beat the egg and stir into the lamb mixture to bind it together, mixing well with a wooden spoon.

3 Turn out the lamb mixture into a 20-cm/8-in flan ring which has been placed on a greased baking tray. Pat the mixture down smoothly with your hand.

4 Sprinkle the garlic and pine nuts over the top of the lamb, and press them gently into the surface of the mixture. Bake in a preheated oven at 180°C, 350°F, Gas Mark 4 for 45 minutes. Serve with cous-cous and roasted peppers.
SERVES: 4

CHILLI CHICKEN

This is a mildly spicy dish, which is best served with plain boiled rice. However, if wished, you can increase the amount of chilli powder.

2 tablespoons oil
4 chicken joints
1 onion, chopped
2 garlic cloves, crushed
1 level teaspoon chilli powder
1 red pepper, seeded and cut into chunks
1 x 400g/14oz can chopped tomatoes
300ml/1/2 pint chicken stock
115g/4oz fresh white breadcrumbs
salt and pepper

1 Heat the oil in a frying pan and brown the chicken joints on both sides. Remove the chicken and set aside. Add onion to the pan, stir and fry for 2 minutes.
2 Add the garlic and chilli powder, and stir-fry for 1-2 minutes, then add the red pepper. Cook for 2 minutes, and then add the tomatoes and the chicken stock. Stir well, and return the chicken pieces to the pan.
3 Cover the pan and simmer until the chicken is cooked, about 30 minutes, depending on the size of the pieces.
4 Remove the cooked chicken, transfer to a serving dish and keep warm.
5 Pour the tomato mixture into a blender or food processor and blend until smooth. Return the sauce to the pan and stir in the breadcrumbs.
6 Heat through gently and check the seasoning. Pour the sauce over the chicken and serve.
SERVES: 4

Tip: the Chilli Chicken can be garnished with colourful rings of red and orange peppers, and sprigs of fresh coriander. To make it even more colourful, you could add some saffron or turmeric.

CHICKEN SAUTÉ

75g/3oz butter
2 large onions, sliced
2 red peppers, seeded and sliced
1 x 1.5kg/3lb chicken
450g/1lb button mushrooms
16 boiled garlic cloves (see note)
1 glass red wine
300ml/1/2 pint thickened chicken stock
20 cooked new potatoes
4 heart-shaped croûtons
chopped fresh parsley
225g/8oz lean back bacon, grilled until crisp and crumbled

1 Heat the butter in a heavy-based frying pan, and add the onions and peppers. Sauté until softened and lightly coloured, and remove.
2 Cut the chicken into eight pieces and chop the bones. Put the chicken pieces and bones into the pan, skin-side down, and cook gently until lightly browned.
3 Stir in the button mushrooms, and return the onions and peppers to the pan. Cover with a lid and cook gently for 5-10 minutes.
4 Remove the white meat joints first, then the dark meat and, finally, the bones. Discard the bones and keep the rest of the meat warm.
5 Add the garlic to the pan and fry gently until coloured. Drain off any excess fat, add the red wine and boil rapidly until reduced.
6 Add the stock and bring to the boil. Stir in the new potatoes and the chicken. Heat through gently.
7 Transfer to a serving dish, and garnish with heart-shaped croûtons with their points dipped in parsley. Sprinkle with bacon and the rest of the parsley and serve.
SERVES: 4

Note: the garlic should be boiled for 7-10 minutes prior to cooking and then cooled before using.

Opposite: Chicken Sauté

COD AND OLIVE SALAD

350g/12oz smoked cod
4 tablespoons olive oil
mixed salad leaves
1 tablespoon white wine vinegar
juice of 1/2 lemon
1 tablespoon capers
4 tomatoes, skinned and chopped
16 black olives, stoned
salt and pepper

1 Place the smoked cod in a bowl and pour 2 tablespoons of the olive oil over the top. Season with salt and pepper, and leave to marinate for 20 minutes.
2 Remove the fish from the marinade and steam for approximately 10 minutes (do not over-cook).
3 Meanwhile, toss the salad leaves in the remaining olive oil and vinegar and arrange on a serving plate. Flake the fish over the top.
4 Squeeze the lemon juice over the fish and sprinkle with the capers, tomatoes and black olives.
SERVES: 4

LENTIL SALAD

350g/12oz green lentils
1 bouquet garni
1 large carrot, diced
1 onion, finely chopped
1 leek, trimmed and finely chopped
115ml/4 fl oz olive oil
3 garlic cloves, crushed
115g/4oz crumbly goat's cheese
1 tablespoon red wine vinegar
1 bunch parsley, finely chopped

1 Wash the lentils thoroughly and put them into a large saucepan. Barely cover the lentils with cold water and add the bouquet garni. Simmer for 10 minutes.

2 Add the vegetables and simmer for a further 10-15 minutes. Do not over-cook them – keep them under-done. Watch the pan and do not let the lentils 'catch'. Add more water if necessary.
3 Drain off the cooking liquid, discard the bouquet garni, and mix the lentils and vegetables carefully with half of the olive oil. Leave to cool.
4 Mix the garlic with the goat's cheese. Add the remaining olive oil and the vinegar and fold in the lentils carefully. Sprinkle with chopped parsley and serve.
SERVES: 4

CAESAR SALAD

1 garlic clove, crushed
1 chopped shallot
1 teaspoon French mustard
1 teaspoon anchovy paste
1 tablespoon fresh lemon juice
1 tablespoon white wine vinegar
1 egg
150ml/1/4 pint olive oil
1 cos or little gem lettuce
6 rashers bacon
3 tablespoons vegetable oil
4 slices bread, crusts removed and diced
50g/2oz grated Parmesan cheese
salt and freshly ground black pepper

1 Put the crushed garlic in a bowl and add chopped shallot, mustard, anchovy paste, lemon juice and wine vinegar. Mix well.
2 Boil some water in a small saucepan and turn off the heat. Place the egg in the water and leave for 4 minutes to coddle. Plunge the egg into cold water, remove the shell, and crush with a fork.
3 Add the egg to the garlic mixture and stir thoroughly. Slowly dribble in the olive oil and season to taste.
4 Separate the leaves of the cos or little gem lettuce and wash well. Shake off any excess water and transfer to a salad bowl. Add the egg mixture and toss well together.

5 Blanch the bacon in boiling water, refresh and cut off the fat. Cut the bacon into thin strips, and pan fry in a little of the vegetable oil until golden brown. Remove and drain on kitchen paper.

6 Pan fry the bread croutons in the remaining vegetable oil until golden. Remove and drain. Sprinkle the croutons and bacon over the salad with the Parmesan cheese, and serve immediately.

SERVES: 4

CHICK PEA & BACON SOUP

225g/8oz chick peas
1.2 litres/2 pints chicken stock
8 rashers streaky bacon
2 tablespoons olive oil
1 large onion, sliced
2 garlic cloves, sliced
3 tablespoons chopped fresh coriander
600ml/1 pint water
good squeeze of lemon juice
salt and freshly ground black pepper
chopped fresh parsley, to garnish

1 Soak the chick peas in some water for 2 days. Drain and put them in a saucepan with the chicken stock, and bring to the boil. Turn down the heat and cook gently for at least 2 hours, until soft. Purée the chick peas with the cooking liquor.

2 Blanch the rashers of bacon in boiling water and then refresh in cold water. Trim off the fat and cut the bacon into thin strips.

3 Heat the olive oil and fry the bacon. Colour lightly, then take out and keep warm. Reserve the oil.

4 Put the oil in a large saucepan, add the sliced onion and garlic and sauté gently until soft and lightly coloured. Add the coriander and water and cook for 10-15 minutes.

5 Purée and then add to the chick pea purée. Season to taste, add some lemon juice and re-heat the soup.

6 Pour the soup into serving bowls and sprinkle with bacon and chopped parsley. Serve hot.

SERVES: 6

BAKED FIELD MUSHROOMS

1 onion, thinly sliced
115ml/4fl oz olive oil
2 courgettes, diced
3 garlic cloves, crushed
8 large field mushrooms, peeled and cleaned
8 small slices mozzarella cheese
2 tablespoons balsamic vinegar
1 tablespoon chopped chives
4 black olives, stoned and chopped
1 little gem lettuce, washed and separated
salt and pepper

1 Sauté the onion in 2 tablespoons of the olive oil until soft until golden. Add the courgettes and garlic and leave to sweat slowly over gentle heat.

2 Place the mushrooms on a buttered grilling tray, underside up, and spoon the onion mixture into the open cups.

3 Cover each one with a small slice of mozzarella and sprinkle with a little olive oil. Season with salt and pepper.

4 Cook in a preheated oven at 200°C, 400°F, Gas Mark 6, until golden brown.

5 Mix the remaining olive oil with the balsamic vinegar, chives and a little salt and pepper. Stir in the chopped olives. Mix with the cooking liquor from the mushrooms.

6 Arrange the lettuce leaves on 4 serving plates and drizzle a little sauce over the top. Place mushrooms on top of the lettuce, cover with the remaining sauce and serve.

SERVES: 4

SALAD DRESSINGS

For a simple, classic French vinaigrette dressing, just mix three parts good olive oil to one part white wine vinegar. Stir in a little Dijon mustard and a pinch of caster sugar. Blend well. If wished, add some chopped herbs or crushed garlic.

CHAPTER FOUR

BUDGET MEALS

Whether you're a student with limited means, on a short-term economy drive or living within tight budgetary guidelines, you can still enjoy delicious meals made from fresh, wholesome ingredients. There are lots of creative recipes in this section to inspire you. All the dishes featured are economical and will fit into your weekly budget.

Chicken with Apples and Cider (see page 57)

KIPPER KEDGEREE

50g/2oz butter
¹/₂ teaspoon curry powder
¹/₂ teaspoon turmeric
1 onion, finely chopped
200g/7oz long-grain rice
400ml/14fl oz water
2 large kippers, skinned, boned and flaked
2 tablespoons chopped fresh parsley
juice and grated zest of ¹/₂ lemon
4 hard-boiled eggs, quartered
salt and pepper

1 Heat the butter in a large frying pan. Add the curry powder and turmeric and fry gently for 1 minute.
2 Add the onion and fry gently until softened and translucent.
3 Add the rice and mix well to coat all the grains in the oil. Pour in the water and bring up to the boil.
4 Simmer for 15-20 minutes, until the rice is just cooked

STANDBY RISOTTO

You can create some delicious dishes with leftovers and standard ingredients from your kitchen cupboards. For a quick, cheap risotto, sauté some onions in a little oil and butter with any vegetables lurking in the refrigerator, e.g. mushrooms, carrots etc. Add the rice and some hot stock together with any leftover meat or fish, some fresh or dried herbs, canned tomatoes or sweetcorn. Cook until the rice is tender and has absorbed all the liquid, topping up as necessary with more stock or even some white wine. Sprinkle with Parmesan and top with a little butter before serving.

and all the liquid has been absorbed. Add more water if necessary.
5 Add the flaked kippers with half of the parsley and the lemon juice and grated zest. Season to taste with salt and pepper and heat through gently.
6 Arrange the quartered hard-boiled eggs on top of the kedgeree and sprinkle with the remaining chopped parsley.
SERVES: 4

TURKISH CIRCASSIAN CHICKEN

4 chicken joints
1 large onion, chopped
1 carrot, chopped
2 tablespoons olive oil
2 garlic cloves, crushed
225g/8oz walnuts, chopped
115g/4oz bread, crusts removed
salt and freshly ground black pepper
paprika, to garnish

1 Put the chicken joints in a saucepan with half the chopped onion and the carrot. Cover with water, bring to the boil and then simmer gently until the chicken is cooked, about 30 minutes.
2 Remove the chicken, reserving the stock. Chop or shred the chicken, discarding the skin and bones.
3 Heat the olive oil and fry the garlic and remaining onion until softened and translucent. Add the chicken meat and a little of the chicken stock to moisten. Season to taste with salt and pepper and heat through gently. Transfer to a serving dish and keep warm.
4 To make the sauce, put the walnuts and bread in a food processor, and process to fine crumbs. Gradually add the reserved stock, a little at a time, until it makes a thick, creamy sauce.
5 Season to taste and pour over the chicken mixture. Serve sprinkled with paprika.
SERVES: 4

CHICKEN WITH APPLES AND CIDER

2 tablespoons oil
4 chicken breasts, skinned
1 level tablespoon plain flour, seasoned with
salt and pepper
1 level teaspoon ground mace
1 garlic clove, crushed
2 tablespoons brown sugar
juice of 1 lemon
300ml/¹/₂ pint cider
2 dessert apples
1 sprig thyme, chopped

1 Heat the oil in a large frying pan. Toss the chicken breasts in the seasoned flour and the mace, then fry in the hot oil with the garlic until golden brown on both sides, turning them halfway through cooking. Remove the chicken and keep warm.

2 Add the sugar to the pan and cook, stirring, for 2-3 minutes until the sugar caramelizes to the colour of toffee.

3 Add the lemon juice and cider, and boil vigorously for a couple of minutes to boil off the alcohol and concentrate the flavour.

4 Return the chicken to the pan and spoon the liquid over the top. Simmer gently, turning occasionally, for about 15 minutes, until the chicken is cooked through.

5 Core the apples and cut into wedges. Add them to the pan, mixing them into the pan juices, and cook briefly, only for 1-2 minutes, to colour and heat the apple without it becoming too soft.

6 Serve sprinkled with chopped fresh thyme.

SERVES: 4

R O B E R T   C A R R I E R

Robert Carrier is internationally recognised as a popular and successful food writer and restaurateur. A television presenter and the author of many best-selling cookery books, he was awarded an OBE in 1987 for his services to the field of catering.

ARANCINI

These little balls of cheese-flavoured saffron rice are deep fried until crisp and golden, then served with a tomato and basil sauce.

2 tablespoons butter
¹/₄ Spanish onion, finely chopped
175g/6oz risotto (Arborio) rice
¹/₂ vegetable stock cube
600ml/1 pint mixed hot vegetable stock and dry white wine
¹/₄ teaspoon powdered saffron
crushed dried chillies, to taste
75g/3oz freshly grated Gruyère cheese
75g/3oz grated Parmesan cheese
salt and freshly ground black pepper

1 Heat the butter in a deep saucepan, add the onion and cook slowly over gentle heat for 2-4 minutes, taking care that the onion does not colour.
2 Add the rice and vegetable stock cube and cook over a medium heat, stirring constantly.
3 After a minute or so, stir in 150ml/¹/₄ pint of the hot vegetable stock and wine to which you have added the powdered saffron. Continue cooking, adding more stock as necessary and stirring from time to time, until the rice is almost cooked (approximately 15 minutes).
4 Season with salt and freshly ground pepper and crushed dried chillies, to taste. Stir in the grated cheese and set aside to cool.
5 When cool, roll the risotto into small balls, about 2cm/³/₄in diameter. Roll each ball in flour, then in beaten egg yolk, and then in dried breadcrumbs.
6 Deep fry the rice balls in hot oil until golden brown, about 3-5 minutes. Remove and drain the Arancini. Serve hot with the Tomato and Basil Sauce (below).
SERVES: 4-6

◆

TOMATO AND BASIL SAUCE

4 tablespoons olive oil
green tops from 6 spring onions, finely chopped
2 x 400g/14oz cans peeled plum tomatoes, drained and chopped
¹/₂ vegetable stock cube, crumbled
12 fresh basil leaves, torn into strips
1 tablespoon chopped fresh parsley
2 teaspoons lemon juice
¹/₂ teaspoon sugar
crushed dried chillies, to taste
salt and freshly ground black pepper

1 Heat the oil in a saucepan. Add the spring onions, tomatoes, the crumbled stock cube, basil, parsley, and lemon juice, and simmer for 5 minutes, stirring from time to time.
2 Season with salt, freshly ground pepper, sugar and crushed dried chillies, to taste.
SERVES: 4

COWBOY BAKED BEANS

25g/1oz butter
1 large onion, chopped
1 garlic clove, crushed
2.5-cm/1-in piece piece fresh root ginger, diced
225g/8oz bacon or ham, diced
2 tablespoons clear honey
1-2 tablespoons Worcestershire sauce
2 x 400g/14oz cans baked beans

1 Melt the butter, add the onion and garlic and cook until soft and translucent. Stir in the ginger and the bacon or ham. Cook without browning for 5 minutes, or until the bacon is cooked through.
2 Add the honey, Worcestershire sauce and baked beans and heat through gently until piping hot. Season to taste and serve with fresh green vegetables or salad.
SERVES: 3-4

CHILLI CON CARNE

Canned kidney beans are quick and convenient to use as they don't need any soaking overnight. Do remember to drain and rinse them first, though, as the liquid in which they are canned has an unpleasant metallic taste. Red kidney beans are high in fibre and rich in protein, and when added to a meat sauce they will create a robust dish.

1 quantity of Tasty Meat Sauce (see page 13)
1-2 teaspoons chilli powder
1 x 300g/10oz can red kidney beans, drained and rinsed
boiled whole-grain rice, to serve

1 Make the Tasty Meat Sauce, adding chilli powder according to taste to the cooked and softened onion and garlic. Cook gently over low heat to release the flavour before adding the bacon and minced beef, then continue as instructed in the recipe.

2 About 20 minutes before the end of the cooking time, stir in the kidney beans and mix thoroughly. Continue cooking until the chilli is piping hot.
3 Serve with nutty whole-grain rice and a crisp green salad.
SERVES: 6

TRIPLE TOMATO PASTA

1 tablespoon vegetable oil
1 onion, chopped
2 garlic cloves, chopped
1 x 400g/14oz can chopped tomatoes
3 tablespoons sundried tomato paste
115g/4oz cherry tomatoes, halved
350g/12oz pasta shapes
150g/5oz feta cheese, cubed
2 tablespoons chopped fresh basil or parsley
salt and pepper

1 Heat the oil in a saucepan, and sauté the onion and garlic until they begin to soften. Add the canned tomatoes, then cook for about 5 minutes, until the sauce has thickened slightly. Stir in the tomato paste and then add the halved cherry tomatoes.
2 Cook the pasta shapes in lightly salted boiling salted water until just tender, then drain and add to the tomato sauce.
3 Season to taste with salt and pepper, and serve with feta cheese. Sprinkle the chopped basil or parsley on top.
SERVES: 4

PASTA

Pasta is a cheap and nutritious food and makes a quick, easy meal. Dried pasta is more economical than the freshly prepared varieties which are now sold in supermarkets. Many pasta devotees think it tastes better, too.

BAKED POTATO TOPPINGS

Baked potatoes make an easy, cheap and nutritious meal. They are extremely versatile and can be filled with various mixtures. Here are some ideas for you to try.

CHINESE-STYLE TOPPING

1 small onion, finely chopped
50g/2oz button mushrooms, finely sliced
1 carrot, cut in thin julienne sticks
50g/2oz water chestnuts, finely sliced
115g/4oz bean sprouts
1 courgette, cut in thin julienne strips
1 tablespoon sesame oil
1 tablespoon yellow bean paste (or soy sauce)

Sauté all the vegetables in the sesame oil for 3-4 minutes until just tender but retaining some bite. Mix in the yellow bean paste or soy sauce and pile into and over the baked jacket potatoes. This is sufficient to fill 4 large potatoes.

RATATOUILLE TOPPING

1 large courgette, sliced
1 aubergine, sliced
3 tablespoons olive oil
1 small onion, chopped
1 garlic clove, crushed
1/2 green pepper, seeded and diced
1/2 red pepper, seeded and diced
2 large tomatoes, skinned and chopped
salt and freshly ground black pepper

1 Put the courgette and aubergine slices in a colander, cover with a plate and weight it down. Leave for 1 hour to press out any excess moisture.
2 Heat the oil in a large frying pan and fry the onion and garlic for 5 minutes over low heat until soft and translucent. Add the peppers and cook gently for 10 minutes. Add all the remaining ingredients and season to taste with salt and pepper.
3 Cover the pan and cook gently over low heat for 35 minutes, stirring from time to time. Use as a filling for 4 large jacket potatoes.

SESAME CHICKEN TOPPING

4 tablespoons dark soy sauce
1 tablespoon orange marmalade
5-mm/1/2-in piece fresh root ginger, peeled and grated
1/2 tablespoon sesame oil
1 garlic clove, crushed
2 chicken breasts, sliced
1 tablespoon sesame seeds

1 Put the soy sauce, orange marmalade, ginger, sesame oil and crushed garlic in a deep bowl and mix well together. Put the sliced chicken in the marinade, ensuring that every slice is well covered. Set aside in a cool place for at least 2 hours, turning the chicken at least once.
2 Put the chicken on a rack over a baking tray and sprinkle with the sesame seeds. Cook in a preheated oven at 220°C, 425°F, Gas Mark 7 for 15 minutes.
3 Remove from the oven and baste with the marinade mixture from the bowl or baking tray. Reduce the oven temperature to 190°C, 375°F, Gas Mark 5 and cook for a further 20-30 minutes. Use as a filling for 4 jacket potatoes.

PASTA WITH TUNA

1 garlic clove, crushed
1 onion, chopped
1 tablespoon vegetable oil
1 small red pepper, seeded and chopped
350g/12oz drained canned tuna
1 x 200g/7oz can sweetcorn, drained
1 tablespoon chopped fresh dill
150ml/5fl oz carton natural yogurt
2 tablespoons single cream
225g/8oz tagliatelle
salt and freshly ground black pepper

1 Sauté the garlic and onion in the oil until softened and translucent. Stir in the pepper and cook gently until the pepper starts to soften.
2 Add the tuna and sweetcorn, then season to taste with dill and salt and pepper. Remove from the heat and stir in the yogurt and cream.
3 Meanwhile, cook the tagliatelle in lightly salted boiling water until just tender. Drain the pasta and then serve with the tuna sauce.
SERVES: 4

BUDGET TIP

For a variation on Frying Pan Pizza, you can make quick individual pizzas using frozen pizza bases or pitta breads. Use one of the toppings suggested (right) or use store cupboard ingredients, e.g. canned pineapple and sweetcorn kernels, sardines or canned salmon. For a more nourishing pizza, break an egg on top of the tomato sauce and cheese, and then grill or oven bake. If you prefer a more traditional style of pizza, turn to the step-by-step recipe on page 32.

FRYING PAN PIZZA

FOR THE DOUGH:
115g/4oz self-raising white flour
115g/4oz wholemeal flour
good pinch of salt
1 level teaspoon dried mixed herbs
1 tablespoon vegetable oil
150ml/¹/₄ pint milk

1 Put the flour, salt and herbs in a mixing bowl. Make a well in the centre, pour in the oil and milk and mix with a wooden spoon until you have a soft ball of dough.
2 Turn out on to a lightly floured surface and knead lightly. Roll or pat out into a circle that will fit your frying pan.
3 Wipe a little oil over the surface of the pan and place it over medium heat. Put the dough in the pan and cook gently for 3-5 minutes until it starts to brown.
4 Turn the dough over and cook the other side for 3-5 minutes. While it is cooking in the pan, prepare one of the suggested toppings.
5 Cover the dough as suggested below and pop under a preheated hot grill for a few minutes.
SERVES: 4

PIZZA TOPPINGS

1 Arrange 3 sliced tomatoes around the edge of the pizza and fill the centre with a small can of tomatoes, drained and mashed with a fork. Add a sprinkling of salt and pepper and 2 crushed garlic cloves, and then top with 115g/4oz grated cheese.
2 Spread some tomato purée generously over the top of the pizza. Season with salt, pepper and garlic, and add a green pepper, seeded and cut into rings, and a few black olives. Sprinkle with some grated cheese or sliced Mozzarella, if wished.
3 Top with tomato slices and canned chopped tomatoes. Drain a small can of tuna and spread the flaked fish over the top. Add grated cheese or sliced Mozzarella, if wished.

HARIRA

This thick, nutritious chick pea soup from Morocco is eaten during Ramadan, the month of fasting. It is served at the end of a day after the sirens sound, signalling that the feasting can begin.

225g/8oz chick peas
225g/8oz chicken leg meat, diced
3 litres/5 pints chicken stock
1 onion, finely chopped
225g/8oz tomatoes, skinned and chopped
1 teaspoon ground cinnamon
115g/4oz vermicelli or long-grain rice
bunch of fresh coriander or parsley, chopped
3 eggs, beaten
salt and freshly ground black pepper
lemon wedges, to serve

1 Soak the chick peas in cold water for 1 hour. Drain and rinse. Place them in a large saucepan with the chicken, stock, onion and tomatoes.
2 Bring to the boil, skimming off any scum that rises to the surface, and add the cinnamon and some ground pepper.
3 Simmer for 1 hour, until the chick peas are tender. Add the vermicelli or rice 15 minutes before the end of the cooking time.
4 Season to taste with salt and pepper, add the coriander or parsley and remove from the heat. Beat the eggs into the hot soup, and serve immediately with lemon wedges.
SERVES: 8

Right: Harira

NORTH AFRICAN FOOD

If you enjoy North African food, you could follow the Harira with the Moroccan Flan (see the step-by-step recipe on page 48). Serve with cous-cous.

SAUSAGES IN CIDER

1 tablespoon vegetable oil
15g/¹/₂oz butter
450g/1lb good quality pork sausages
1 large onion, thinly sliced
1 x 400g/14oz can red kidney beans, drained and rinsed
1 x 400g/14oz can chopped tomatoes
¹/₂ teaspoon crushed, dried chilli flakes
2 tablespoons tomato purée
300ml/¹/₂ pint dry cider
salt and pepper

1 Heat the oil and butter in a flameproof casserole dish. Sauté the sausages for about 5 minutes until browned all over. Remove and cut each sausage in half lengthways.
2 Add the onion to the casserole and cook gently until softened and translucent.
3 Return the sausages to the casserole dish, together with the beans, tomatoes, chilli flakes, tomato purée, cider, and salt and pepper to taste. Cover and cook gently for about 25 minutes, or until the sausages are tender. Serve with puréed potatoes and red cabbage.
SERVES: 4

GRILLED BELLY OF PORK WITH HORSERADISH MUSTARD

1 x 675g/1¹/₂lb belly of pork
25g/1oz butter
1 carrot, sliced
1 onion, chopped
1 stick celery, chopped
1 bulb of garlic, cut in half
4 tomatoes, halved
300ml/¹/₂ pint dry white wine
1.2 litres/2 pints brown stock
few sprigs of parsley and thyme
50g/2oz horseradish mustard
225g/8oz fresh breadcrumbs
puréed swede and carrot, to serve
salt and freshly ground black pepper

1 Sear the outside of the belly of pork in a frying pan in the hot butter, until browned all over. Place in a large deep roasting dish.
2 In the same frying pan, colour the carrot, onion and celery, and then add these to the meat in the roasting dish, together with the garlic, tomatoes, wine and brown stock.
3 Add the herbs and cover and bake in a preheated oven at 160°C, 325°F, Gas Mark 3, for 2-3 hours.
4 Reserving the cooking liquor, remove the meat and slip the bones out. Leave the meat to cool with a weight on top. When cold, cut diagonally into strips, 1cm/¹/₂in wide. Brush with horseradish mustard and beaten egg, and sprinkle with breadcrumbs.
5 Put in a roasting pan in the oven at 180°C, 350°F, Gas Mark 4, to re-heat thoroughly. Finish them under the grill to brown them and arrange on a bed of puréed swede and carrot.
6 Strain the cooking liquor into a saucepan, bring to the boil and serve with the meat.
SERVES: 4

Opposite: Sausages in Cider

HERBY MINCE AND POTATO PIE

1 onion, finely chopped
50ml/2fl oz olive oil
450g/1lb minced beef or lamb
10 tomatoes, skinned, seeded and chopped
3 cloves garlic, crushed
1 glass red wine
300ml/¹/₂ pint beef stock
675g/1¹/₂lb potatoes
1 bunch parsley, chopped
few sprigs of basil, chopped unsalted butter
50ml/2fl oz milk
1 egg, beaten
salt and pepper

1 Sweat the onions in 25ml/1fl oz of the olive oil, without colouring. Remove the onions and set aside.
2 Add the mince to the hot oil and cook for a few minutes, stirring occasionally until lightly browned.
3 Return the onions to the pan, add the tomatoes and 1 clove of crushed garlic, and stew gently for 10 minutes.
4 Stir in the wine and cook rapidly until reduced. Add the stock and simmer gently until the meat is cooked.
5 Boil hard to reduce the stock so that the meat is fairly stiff in texture. Season to taste, transfer to a pie dish and set aside to go cold.
6 Meanwhile, boil the potatoes until tender and then drain and purée them. Put the parsley, basil and the rest of the garlic in a food processor with the rest of the olive oil and blend well. Mix into the puréed potatoes with the warm milk. Season to taste and leave to cool.
7 Pipe the potato in swirls over the top of the pie. Bake in a preheated oven at 180°C, 350°F, Gas Mark 4 for 10 minutes. Remove the pie, brush with beaten egg and return to the oven. Increase the temperature to 200°C, 400°F, Gas Mark 6, and bake in the middle of the oven for about 30 more minutes, until crisp and golden brown. Serve the pie immediately with green vegetables of your choice.
SERVES: 4

BOBOTIE

This traditional South African dish can be made with leftover meat, which has been finely chopped or minced. Although it is usually lamb, you could use beef. If using fresh mince, cook it first by frying in a little oil for 15 minutes, stirring frequently to prevent it forming lumps.

1 tablespoon vegetable oil
1 onion, chopped
1-2 tablespoons curry powder
1 apple, peeled, cored and diced
1 large slice white bread
3 tablespoons milk
2 tablespoons apricot chutney
25g/1oz raisins
1 tablespoon lemon juice
750g/1lb 10oz minced cooked lamb
2 eggs, beaten
300ml/¹/₂ pint plain yogurt
25g/1oz flaked almonds
6 bay leaves
salt and freshly ground black pepper

1 In a large pan, heat the oil and fry the onion until soft and translucent. Add the curry powder, stirring well, and fry gently for a few minutes. Stir in the apple and cook for 2-3 minutes.
2 Soak the bread in the milk. While it is soaking, add the chutney, raisins and lemon juice to the onion in the pan. Season with salt and pepper and mix in the lamb.
3 Squeeze the excess milk out of the bread and mix the bread into the meat mixture.
4 Transfer to a shallow ovenproof dish and smooth the surface.
5 Beat the eggs together and then beat them into the yogurt. Pour over the meat mixture and scatter the flaked almonds and bay leaves over the top.
6 Bake in a preheated oven at 180°C, 350°F, Gas Mark 4 for 35 minutes, until the topping is crisp. Serve with rice, poppadums and sambals.
SERVES: 4-6

ROASTED BACON WITH LENTIL AND CARROT STEW

1.8kg/4lb collar of bacon
1 bay leaf
6 peppercorns
English mustard
115g/4oz white breadcrumbs
50g/2oz brown sugar
1 onion, chopped
2 tablespoons olive oil
225g/8oz lentils
1.5 litres/2 1/2 pints chicken stock
450g/1lb carrots, peeled
450g/1lb potatoes, peeled and quartered
oil for roasting
few sprigs of fresh coriander, chopped
salt and pepper

1 Soak the bacon joint in cold water for about 2 hours. Drain and place in a saucepan with the bay leaf and peppercorns, cover with fresh water and boil for 2 hours.
2 Remove the bacon joint from the pan and strip off the rind. Brush the top with mustard. Mix the sugar and breadcrumbs together and use to coat the bacon, patting it down firmly.
3 Bake in a preheated oven at 200°C, 400°F, Gas Mark 6 for 20 minutes, then lower the heat to 180°C, 350°F, Gas Mark 4, for approximately 40 minutes, until the bacon is crisp on the outside.
4 Meanwhile, sweat the onion in the olive oil until softened, without colouring.
5 Add the lentils and the chicken stock. Bring to the boil, then simmer until cooked, approximately 20 minutes, being careful not to let it boil dry.
6 Cut the carrots into batons and boil in lightly salted water until tender. Drain, then pour into lentils and mix together gently. Season to taste.
7 Meanwhile, blanch the potatoes, drain and roast them in oil.
8 Pour the lentil mixture into a dish and slice the bacon over the top. Surround with the roasted potatoes, sprinkled with coriander.
SERVES: 4

RICHARD'S TUNA CASSEROLE

This is the dish that Richard used to make for Judy before they were married. Not only is it economical, it's also very quick and easy to prepare.

1 x 200ml/7fl oz can mushroom soup
1 x 200g/7oz can tuna, drained
1 x 200g/7oz can sweetcorn kernels, drained
1/4 teaspoon dried mixed herbs
115g/4oz button mushrooms, halved
50g/2oz shelled prawns
1 bay leaf

115ml/4fl oz white wine (optional)
freshly ground black pepper
2 packets salted crisps, crushed

FOR THE TOPPING:
2 packets salted crisps, crushed

In a large ovenproof dish, mix together all the ingredients. Top with more crushed crisps, then bake in a preheated oven at 180°C, 350°F, Gas Mark 4 for 20 minutes.
SERVES: 3-4

CHAPTER FIVE

VEGETARIAN FOOD

You don't have to be a vegetarian to enjoy the healthy meals in this chapter. There are unusual flans and pies, salads, gratins and vegetable bakes as well as elegant appetizers, such as Goat's Cheese Darioles. Try them and discover how delicious vegetarian food can be.

Crispy Leek and Cheese Flan (see page 70)

CRISPY LEEK AND CHEESE FLAN

25g/1oz butter
2 garlic cloves, crushed
1.3kg/3lb leeks, trimmed and thinly sliced
2 large eggs
300ml/¹/₂ pint natural yogurt
50g/2oz Caerphilly cheese, grated
salt and freshly ground black pepper

FOR THE PASTRY:
115g/4oz butter, softened
225g/8oz plain flour (or half plain white and half wholemeal)
¹/₂ teaspoon dry mustard powder
pinch of salt
50g/2oz Cheddar cheese, grated
cold water, to mix

1 Make the pastry. Rub the butter into the flour until the mixture resembles fine breadcrumbs. Stir in the mustard powder, salt and grated Cheddar. Mix with sufficient cold water to form a soft but not sticky dough.
2 Roll out on a lightly floured surface and use to line a greased 25-cm/10-in flan ring. Lightly prick the base with a fork. Fill with crumpled greaseproof paper and baking beans, and bake 'blind' in a preheated oven at 180°C, 350°F, Gas Mark 4 for 10-15 minutes.
3 Remove the paper and beans, increase the oven temperature to 190°C, 375°F, Gas Mark 5 and return to the oven for 5 minutes to crisp up the base.
4 For the filling, melt the butter in a large frying pan and add the garlic and leeks. Cook gently for 10-15 minutes, without browning them. Drain off any liquid and leave to cool slightly.
5 Beat the eggs and whisk in the yogurt. Season with salt and pepper and then fold in the Caerphilly and leeks, stirring well.
6 Pour into the flan case and return to the oven for 30-35 minutes, until set and golden brown. Serve with a crisp green salad and jacket potatoes.
SERVES: 6

BEAN PROVENCAL

225g/8oz mixed beans, e.g. red kidney beans, pinto beans, black-eyed beans, haricot beans
1 onion, chopped
1 garlic clove, crushed
2 tablespoons vegetable oil
300ml/¹/₂ pint vegetable stock
1 x 400g/14oz can chopped tomatoes
1 teaspoon chopped fresh tarragon
1 tablespoon lemon juice
1 tablespoon tomato purée
115g/4oz button mushrooms
225g/8oz chopped green pepper
3 tablespoons chopped fresh parsley
salt and pepper

1 Soak the beans in water overnight, then rinse well and drain. Alternatively, boil them for 10 minutes, drain and soak in cold water for 20 minutes. Rinse and drain.
2 Sauté the beans with the onion and garlic in the oil for a few minutes. Add the stock, tomatoes, tarragon, lemon juice and tomato purée. Simmer for 50 minutes until the beans

are cooked. Alternatively, pressure-cook them for 20 minutes.
3 Add the button mushrooms and green pepper, and cook for a further 3 minutes. Season to taste and stir in the parsley.
4 Serve the beans with a green salad and some wholemeal bread or jacket potatoes.
SERVES: 4

PETER JONES'S AUBERGINE BAKE

3 medium aubergines, sliced
flour for coating
1 garlic clove, crushed
50ml/2fl oz sunflower oil
1 small onion, chopped
1 x 400g/14oz can chopped tomatoes, drained
1 tablespoon tomato purée
few leaves of basil, chopped
2 packets Mozzarella cheese
25g/1oz grated Parmesan cheese
25g/1oz fresh white breadcrumbs
salt and pepper

1 Lay the aubergine slices in a colander and sprinkle the layers with salt. Leave for 1 hour to exude their bitter juices.
2 Pat dry with kitchen paper and coat with flour by shaking inside a plastic bag.
3 Fry them with the garlic in the oil until golden brown on both sides. Remove from the pan and drain on kitchen paper.
4 Fry the onion in the same oil until soft and translucent.
5 Mix the fried onion with the tomatoes, tomato purée and basil. If wished, blend in a food processor or liquidizer. Season to taste.
6 Layer up the aubergine, mozzarella and tomato sauce in a soufflé dish, starting with a layer of aubergine and finishing with the tomato sauce. Sprinkle with Parmesan and breadcrumbs.
7 Bake in a preheated oven at 180°C, 350°F, Gas Mark 4 for 30-40 minutes, until golden brown. Serve with brown rice.
SERVES: 4

BASIC WHITE SAUCE

25g/1oz butter or margarine
25g/1oz plain flour
300ml/¹/₂ pint milk
salt and pepper

1 Melt the butter or margarine in a saucepan and stir in the flour. Cook gently for 1 minute over low heat, without browning.
2 Gradually add the milk, stirring continuously with a wire whisk, until the sauce boils and thickens.
3 Reduce the heat and simmer for 5 minutes. Season with salt and pepper. If wished, you could add grated nutmeg, cheese, parsley or other herbs to flavour the sauce.
MAKES: 300ml/¹/₂ pint

TABBOULEH

150g/5oz bulgar wheat
1 large bunch parsley, chopped
4 sprigs of mint, chopped
3 tomatoes, skinned and chopped
3 tablespoons olive oil
juice of 1 lemon
lettuce leaves, to garnish
salt and pepper

1 Put the bulgar wheat in a bowl and cover with cold water – the water level should be 2.5 cm/1 in above the bulgar wheat. Leave to soak for 2 hours, until it has absorbed most of the water.
2 Tip into a sieve and squeeze the bulgar wheat to drain off the excess water. Transfer to a clean bowl.
3 Mix the bulgar wheat with the chopped herbs, tomatoes, olive oil and lemon juice, and season to taste. Serve on a bed of lettuce leaves.
SERVES: 4-6

CHEESE, POTATO AND SPINACH PIE

450g/1lb fresh spinach
3 bunches spring onions, finely chopped
2 large potatoes
115g/4oz butter
2 onions, chopped
2 eggs, beaten
115g/4oz feta cheese
1 packet of filo pastry
salt and freshly ground black pepper

1 Pick the spinach over, removing the stems. Wash and drain well, then chop finely. Place in a bowl with the spring onions.
2 Peel and slice the potatoes and cut them into rounds about 5mm/¹/₄in thick. Sauté in a little of the butter to colour them and then cook slowly over low heat until tender with just a little bite. Remove from the pan and set aside to cool.
3 Sauté the chopped onions in some of the remaining butter until they soften.
4 Add the fried onions, beaten eggs, some salt and lots of freshly ground pepper to the spinach and spring onions. Gently mix in the feta cheese.
5 Melt the remaining butter and use some of it to grease a 20-cm/8-in round deep flan tin. Place a layer of filo pastry in the base of the tin with the edges overhanging the edge. Brush with butter and then add another two or three layers of filo pastry, each one brushed with butter, to form a crust for the pie.
6 Arrange the potatoes in the bottom and pour the spinach filling over the top. Fold the overhanging edges of pastry over into the middle and brush with melted butter. Finish the pie by covering with some more layers of filo pastry, brushing with butter between the layers once again.
7 Bake in a preheated oven at 170°C, 325°F, Gas Mark 3, for 40 minutes. Allow to rest before serving.
SERVES: 4

GOAT'S CHEESE DARIOLES

25g/1oz butter
1 shallot, chopped
¹/₂ garlic clove, crushed
few sprigs parsley, chopped
6 tomatoes, skinned, seeded and diced
25g/1oz fresh breadcrumbs
75ml/3fl oz warm milk
175g/6oz goat's cheese
200ml/7fl oz double cream
5 egg yolks
squeeze of lemon juice
salad leaves, to garnish
1 tablespoon olive oil
1 teaspoon balsamic vinegar
salt and pepper

1 Melt the butter and sauté the shallot until softened. Add the garlic, parsley and half of the diced tomatoes. Season with salt and pepper, and remove from the heat.
2 Soak the breadcrumbs in the warm milk, stir in the goat's cheese and then blend in a food processor. Add the double cream, egg yolks and lemon juice, and blend together. Season to taste with salt and pepper and mix with the tomato mixture.
3 Butter 6 dariole moulds and fill with the cheese and tomato mixture. Stand the moulds in a roasting pan half-filled with water, and cook in a preheated oven at 170°C, 325°F, Gas Mark 3 for about 20 minutes, until they are set.
4 Turn out the darioles and garnish with salad leaves. Mix the remaining tomatoes with the oil and vinegar, season and pour around the darioles.
SERVES: 6

Variation: serve the Goat's Cheese Darioles with a fresh tomato coulis. Just skin and seed some ripe tomatoes and purée them. Season with salt and pepper and a pinch of caster sugar and some finely chopped herbs.

Opposite: Goat's Cheese Darioles

COURGETTE GRATIN

75g/3oz butter
450g/1lb courgettes
225g/8oz cooked rice
150ml/¹/4 pint béchamel sauce (see opposite)
salt and pepper

1 Melt 50g/2oz of the butter in a frying pan and gently sweat the courgettes, to soften them. Do not brown them.
2 Purée them in a food processor or blender. Transfer to a bowl and mix in the cooked rice and béchamel sauce. Season to taste.
3 With the remaining butter, grease an ovenproof dish and fill with the courgette mixture. Bake in a preheated oven at 200°C, 400°F, Gas Mark 6, for about 20 minutes, until lightly browned.
SERVES: 4

BAKED STUFFED MUSHROOMS

4 large field mushrooms, peeled and stalks removed
115g/4oz goat's cheese
1 egg yolk
2 bacon rashers, cut into strips and fried until crispy
450g/1lb boiled new potatoes, halved
2 tablespoons consommé
¹/2 onion, chopped
1 tablespoon mayonnaise
juice of ¹/2 lemon
4 tablespoons olive oil
2 tablespoons chopped fresh chives
freshly ground black pepper

1 Put a splash of the olive oil into a hot frying pan, add the mushrooms, black side down, and cook for 2 minutes. Turn over and cook for a further 2 minutes. Remove and drain on absorbent kitchen paper.

2 In a bowl, mix the goat's cheese with the egg yolk, and mix in the crisply fried bacon strips. Fill the mushrooms with this mixture and place in a baking dish.
3 Cook in a preheated oven at 180°C, 350°F, Gas Mark 4, for 6 minutes.
4 Soak the warm cooked new potatoes in the warm consommé. Add the onion and mayonnaise and mix gently together, then season to taste with salt and pepper. Pile on to 4 serving plates and put a stuffed mushroom on top of each one.
5 Mix the lemon juice with the remaining olive oil and season with pepper. Pour over the mushrooms and serve sprinkled with chopped chives.
SERVES: 4

GLAMORGAN SAUSAGES

115g/4oz white breadcrumbs
50g/2oz white of leek
3 tablespoons chopped fresh parsley
150g/5oz Caerphilly cheese, grated
2 sprigs fresh thyme
pinch of mustard powder
1 egg yolk
1 egg, beaten
fresh white breadcrumbs, for coating
oil for shallow frying
salt and pepper

1 In a food processor, combine the breadcrumbs, leek and parsley into a fine crumb mixture. Add the cheese, thyme and mustard powder. Add the egg yolk to bind, and season with salt and pepper.
2 Form the mixture into sausage shapes, using your hands. Pass through the beaten egg and then coat with the breadcrumbs.
3 Shallow fry the 'sausages' in hot oil, turning them occasionally, until golden brown and cooked. Drain off any excess fat on absorbent kitchen paper and serve with a crisp green salad.
SERVES: 4

ALLIUM TART

Onions, garlic, and chives are all related, and part of the allium family. This explains the name of this delicious quiche, which puts together three of the cousins.

FOR THE PASTRY:
50g/2oz self-raising flour
50g/2oz wholemeal flour
1/4 teaspoon salt
50g/2oz butter
40g/1½oz grated cheese
cold water, to mix

FOR THE FILLING:
50g/2oz butter
700g/1½lb mixed red and white onions, thinly sliced
1 garlic clove, crushed
2 tablespoons chopped fresh chives
2 eggs, beaten
115ml/4fl oz double cream or Greek yogurt
50g/2oz grated cheese
salt and freshly ground black pepper

1 Make the pastry. Put the flours and salt in a mixing bowl and rub in the butter until the mixture resembles fine breadcrumbs.
2 Stir in the grated cheese, and then add just enough cold water to bind to a soft but not sticky dough. Wrap in a polythene bag or cling film, and leave in the refrigerator to chill while you make the filling.
3 Melt the butter in a pan, add the garlic and onions and leave to cook gently without a lid for about 30 minutes, stirring from time to time to prevent sticking. They should turn dark brown in this time – if they don't, turn up the heat and stir continuously until they colour.
4 Roll out the chilled pastry to line a 20-cm/8-in flan tin, prick the base with a fork, and bake for 15 minutes in a preheated oven at 180°C, 350°F, Gas Mark 4.
5 Take out of the oven and brush the base of the pastry case with a little beaten egg (use the eggs needed for the filling for this; you won't need very much eggwash) and then put the pastry back in the oven for another 5 minutes.

Remove from the oven, and spread the cooked brown onion mixture over the base.
6 Mix the chives with the beaten eggs. Season with salt and freshly ground black pepper to taste, and stir in the double cream or Greek yogurt. Pour carefully over the onions in the pastry case – it should just fill the case, if the onion mixture reduced sufficiently. Take care not to let any of the filling spill over the top.
7 Sprinkle with the grated cheese, and bake in the oven at the same temperature for 30 minutes, until the filling is golden brown and risen. Serve hot or cold.
SERVES: 4-6

BECHAMEL SAUCE

600ml/1 pint milk
1 onion, studded with 1 clove
25g/1oz butter
25g/1oz flour
salt and pepper

1 Place the milk in a saucepan with the clove-studded onion. Bring to the boil, then reduce the heat and simmer gently for 5 minutes.
2 Remove from the heat, cover the pan and leave to infuse for 15 minutes. Strain and discard the onion and clove.
3 Melt the butter and stir in the flour. Cook gently for 1 minute, then gradually beat in the strained milk, beating and stirring until the sauce is smooth, thick and glossy. When it starts to bubble, reduce the heat and simmer gently for 5 minutes. Season with salt and pepper to taste, and use the sauce as required.
MAKES: 600ml/1 pint

GREEN PASTA WITH NUT SAUCE

1 garlic clove, sliced
1 tablespoon fresh white breadcrumbs
150g/5oz toasted hazelnuts or walnuts
50g/2oz grated Pecerino or Parmesan cheese
1 tablespoon chopped fresh oregano (or 1 teaspoon dried)
6 tablespoons olive oil
4 tablespoons Greek yogurt
450g/1lb fresh green fettucine or tagliatelle
salt and freshly ground black pepper

1 Pound the garlic in a mortar with the breadcrumbs, nuts, grated cheese, oregano and salt and pepper. Slowly add the oil, in a thin stream, stirring all the time until the sauce thickens and amalgamates. Stir in the yogurt. If preferred, the sauce can be made in a food processor.
2 Cook the pasta in lightly salted boiling water until just tender, then drain well. Toss the hot pasta in the sauce, and serve immediately.
SERVES: 4

SESAME AND BROCCOLI PASTA

175g/6oz fusilli, or pasta shapes
4 teaspoons sesame oil
6 spring onions, chopped
2 teaspoons minced chilli
175g/6oz button mushrooms
1 tablespoon liquid honey
2 tablespoons dark soy sauce
175g/6oz broccoli florets, blanched for 1 minute in boiling water
3 teaspoons sesame seeds
salt and freshly ground black pepper

1 Cook the pasta in boiling salted water until it is just cooked, then drain and set aside.
2 Heat a wok, or large frying pan, and add the sesame oil. Add the spring onions and stir-fry quickly in the hot oil for about 1 minute.
3 Add the minced chilli and stir-fry quickly, then add the mushrooms. Mix well, add the honey and soy sauce, and then the blanched florets of broccoli.
4 Stir well together and add the cooked and drained pasta. Season to taste and serve sprinkled with sesame seeds.
SERVES: 4

TAGLIATELLE WITH BEANS AND RICOTTA

50g/2oz butter
1 garlic clove, crushed
115g/4oz pancetta or gammon, cut into strips
1 x 400g/14oz can cannellini beans, drained
200g/7oz ricotta cheese, crumbled
150ml/5fl oz single cream
2 tablespoons milk
450g/1lb fresh tagliatelle
4 tablespoons grated Parmesan cheese
salt and freshly ground black pepper

1 Heat the butter in a large saucepan and sauté the garlic quickly until golden. Add the pancetta or gammon and sauté for 2 minutes.
2 Reduce the heat, add the beans and cook for 5 minutes. Add the ricotta and cream, stirring until smooth. Cook very gently for 5 minutes, stirring constantly. Add the milk and seasoning to taste and cook gently for 2 minutes.
3 Meanwhile, cook the pasta in some lightly salted boiling water until just tender. Drain well and then tip into the sauce and mix thoroughly. Serve immediately, sprinkled with Parmesan and plenty of freshly ground black pepper.
SERVES: 4

Opposite: Sesame and Broccoli Pasta

STEW OF FENNEL AND TOMATOES

450g/1lb fennel, trimmed and shredded
25g/1oz butter
1 garlic clove, crushed
1 x 400g/14oz can chopped tomatoes, strained and juice reserved
300ml/¹/₂ pint white sauce (see page 71)
1 egg yolk
115g/4oz Lancashire cheese, grated
50g/2oz fresh breadcrumbs
salt and freshly ground black pepper

1 Sweat the fennel in the butter for about 2 minutes, until softened. Add the garlic and tomatoes, and reduce by cooking until slightly thickened.
2 Warm the white sauce and beat in the egg yolk. Season to taste and stir in the grated cheese.
3 Transfer the fennel and tomato stew to an ovenproof dish, pour the cheese sauce over the top and sprinkle with breadcrumbs. Bake in a preheated oven at 180°C, 350°F, Gas Mark 4, for 15 minutes until golden brown.
SERVES: 4

POTATO PANCAKES

250g/9oz potatoes, peeled and quartered
75g/3oz flour
2 eggs, beaten
1 egg white
25ml/1fl oz double cream
25ml/1fl oz milk
2 tablespoons chopped fresh parsley
oil for shallow frying
salt and pepper

1 Steam the potatoes until cooked, then push through the fine holes in a mincing machine into a bowl and cool.
2 Mix the flour, beaten eggs, egg white, cream, milk and seasoning. Combine with the potatoes, then pass through a sieve and add the chopped parsley. Form into small patties.
3 Fry the potato cakes, a few at a time, in a little oil in a non-stick pan until golden on both sides.
4 Remove and keep warm while you cook the remaining potato cakes.
SERVES: 4

SWEETCORN PANCAKES WITH AVOCADO

50g/2oz plain flour
pinch of salt
1 egg, beaten
150ml/¹/₄ pint milk
115g/4oz canned sweetcorn kernels, drained
1 avocado, peeled, stoned and chopped
juice of ¹/₂ small lemon
4 tomatoes, chopped
1 red onion, finely chopped
1 tablespoon olive oil
50ml/2fl oz natural yogurt
salt and pepper

1 Sieve the flour and salt into a bowl and make a 'well' in the centre. Put the egg and milk into the 'well' and mix with the flour. Beat until smooth and leave to rest. Strain, then add the sweetcorn.
2 Sprinkle the avocado with the lemon juice. Mix in the tomatoes and onion, and season to taste with salt and pepper.
3 Heat a little of the oil in a small frying pan, add some batter and swirl around. Cook gently until golden underneath and then flip over and cook the other side. Remove the pancake and repeat with the remaining batter.
4 Pile the avocado mixture on top of the pancakes, and top with a teaspoonful of yogurt.
SERVES: 4

Opposite: Sweetcorn Pancakes with Avocado

STOVIES WITH MUSHROOMS

Using this method, potatoes can be layered with mushrooms and then baked slowly in the oven.

1 tablespoon oil
115g/4oz softened butter
1kg/2lb potatoes, peeled and finely sliced
1lb/500g mushrooms, sliced
salt and pepper

1 Heat the oil and half of the butter in a flameproof dish. Add the potatoes and toss over a high heat to seal them. Remove half from the pan and spread on the bottom of the dish.
2 Cover with the mushrooms and add some more butter, then cover with a layer of the remaining potatoes. Sprinkle the top with more butter and season with salt and pepper.
3 Cook in a preheated oven at 180°C, 350°F, Gas Mark 4 for about 30 minutes. Towards the end of the cooking time, sprinkle with a little more butter. If necessary, cover the dish with buttered greaseproof paper. The top should be golden and the potatoes cooked and soft.
SERVES: 4-6

COURGETTE AND RAISIN SALAD

450g/1lb baby courgettes
3 tablespoons olive oil
2 garlic cloves, crushed
25g/1oz pine nuts
50g/2oz raisins
juice of 1/2 lemon
salt and freshly ground black pepper

1 Trim the courgettes and cut into into 2.5-cm/1-in pieces. Plunge them into boiling water for 1 minute, then drain.
2 Heat the oil and add the courgettes. Colour them lightly.

Season and add the garlic, pine nuts and raisins.
3 Sprinkle with lemon juice and leave to cool before serving.
SERVES: 4

GREEN BEAN SALAD

450g/1lb French fine green beans, trimmed
3 tablespoons olive or walnut oil
1 tablespoon white wine vinegar
115g/4oz Roquefort or blue cheese
50g/2oz chopped walnuts
salt and pepper
salad leaves

1 Plunge the beans into boiling salted water and cook until 'al dente'. Refresh in iced water, then drain and dry.
2 Mix together the oil and vinegar and season with salt and pepper. Crumble in the cheese and chopped walnuts.
3 Toss the cooked beans in the cheese and walnut dressing.
4 Arrange some salad leaves on each serving plate. Carefully pile some of the beans on top and serve.
SERVES: 4

COLESLAW

450g/1lb white cabbage, thinly sliced
1 onion, finely chopped
2 carrots, grated
1 apple, peeled, cored and grated
3 tablespoons mayonnaise
juice of 1 lemon
salt and pepper

1 In a large bowl, mix together the cabbage, onion, carrots and apple.
2 Mix the mayonnaise with the lemon juice and stir into the cabbage mixture. Season with salt and pepper.
SERVES: 4

R O B E R T   C A R R I E R

Robert Carrier is internationally recognised as a popular and successful food writer and restaurateur. A television presenter and the author of many best-selling cookery books, he was awarded an OBE in 1987 for his services to the field of catering.

POLENTINI

These are flat squares or circles of fried polenta, which are topped with thinly sliced mushrooms in a cream sauce. You should prepare the polenta in advance.

6 tablespoons butter
4 tablespoons finely chopped onion
750ml/1¼ pints water
175g/6oz instant polenta
crushed dried chillies, to taste
olive oil, for brushing
oil for deep frying
salt and freshly ground black pepper
salad leaves, watercress and black olives, to garnish

1 In a medium-sized saucepan, melt 2 tablespoons of the butter and sauté the onion, stirring over gentle heat until softened and transparent.
2 Add the water and bring to a fast simmer. Trickle in the polenta in a thin stream, stirring all the while. Bring slowly to the boil again, then reduce the heat and simmer for 5 minutes, stirring constantly.
3 Beat in the remaining butter, and add the salt, freshly ground pepper and the crushed dried chillies, to taste.
4 Pour the mixture into an oiled rectangular baking tin, spread to a thickness of 1 cm/½ in. Allow to cool.
5 When cold, turn the polenta out of the tin and cut into squares or circles about 4 cm/1½ in diameter. Deep fry the polenta in hot oil for approximately 3-5 minutes, until golden. Remove and drain. Spoon the Mushroom Sauce over the polenta and serve garnished with salad leaves, watercress and black olives.
SERVES: 6

MUSHROOM SAUCE
few slices of dried porcini mushrooms (optional)
2 tablespoons butter
1-2 shallots, finely chopped
2 cloves garlic, crushed
1 vegetable stock cube, crumbled
115g/4oz mushrooms, finely sliced
115g/4oz oyster mushrooms, finely sliced
150ml/¼ pint creme fraîche
1 tablespoon chopped fresh parsley
salt and freshly ground black pepper
crushed dried chillies, to taste

1 Place the porcini (dried mushrooms) in a small bowl and cover with boiling water. Let the mushrooms steep in the water until soft. Strain off the water and squeeze any excess water out.
2 Heat the butter in a frying pan and add the shallots and garlic. Cook gently, stirring occasionally, until the shallots are transparent.
3 Add the vegetable stock cube and stir well into the shallot mixture. Add the fresh mushrooms and porcini, and cook until tender.
4 Stir in the creme fraîche and heat through gently. Add the parsley, salt, freshly ground pepper, and crushed dried chillies, to taste.
SERVES: 6

CHAPTER SIX

INTERNATIONAL FLAVOURS

◆

In the following pages, there are some colourful dishes from around the world, especially the Far East and the Caribbean. Now that supermarkets stock so many exotic foods, it is possible to prepare a wide range of exciting oriental meals in your own home. There is no need to eat out or order in a takeaway meal when you can cook it yourself.

Pork and Chicken Satay (see page 84)

PORK AND CHICKEN SATAY

450g/1lb pork fillet, cubed
450g/1lb chicken breasts, skinned, boned and cubed

FOR THE PORK MARINADE:
1/2 onion, finely chopped
1 garlic clove, crushed
1 teaspoon Chinese five-spice powder
2.5-cm/1-in piece fresh root ginger, peeled and finely
chopped
2 tablespoons light soy sauce
1 tablespoon clear honey

INDONESIAN SOY RELISH

3 tablespoons sesame oil
1 onion, finely chopped
2 garlic cloves, crushed
1/2 teaspoon chilli powder
6 tablespoons dark soy sauce
3 tablespoons cider or wine vinegar
2 heaped teaspoons sugar
2 heaped teaspoons dried lemon grass
3 tablespoons cold water
salt, to taste

1 Heat the sesame oil in a saucepan and fry the onion and garlic, until the onion is translucent and softened and beginning to brown.
2 Add all the other ingredients and cook together, stirring, for a few minutes.
3 Pour into a serving dish, and serve at room temperature with the satay. This sauce will keep fresh for several days in a screwtop jar in the refrigerator.

---

2 tablespoons vegetable oil
1 teaspoon dried lemon grass

FOR THE CHICKEN MARINADE:
50g/2oz creamed coconut, grated
150ml/1/4 pint hot water
2.5-cm/1-in piece fresh root ginger, peeled and finely
chopped
2 garlic cloves, crushed
2 teaspoons ground coriander
1/2 teaspoon ground ginger
2 teaspoons vegetable oil

1 Blend together all the ingredients for the pork marinade. Add the pork, turning the cubes over in the marinade to coat them, and leave in a cool place to marinate for 2 hours.
2 Meanwhile, make the chicken marinade. Mix the creamed coconut with the hot water to form a smooth paste, and then stir in the remaining ingredients. Add the chicken and leave to marinate for 2 hours.
3 Thread the marinated pork onto wooden satay sticks, and then thread the chicken onto wooden sticks. Barbecue or grill, turning occasionally to cook evenly, until the pork and chicken are cooked. Serve with Peanut Sauce or Indonesian Soy Relish.
SERVES: 6-8

TERIYAKI CHICKEN

4 chicken joints
4 tablespoons orange marmalade
4 tablespoons teriyaki sauce or soy sauce
toasted sesame seeds, to garnish
few sprigs parsley, chopped, to garnish
fine threads of orange zest (optional)

1 Place the chicken joints in a baking pan. Mix the marmalade and teriyaki or soy sauce together, then pour over the chicken and leave to marinate for 20 minutes.
2 Bake the chicken in a preheated oven at 190°C, 375°F,

Gas Mark 5 for 20-30 minutes, until the chicken is thoroughly cooked, using the marinade to baste.

3 Serve the chicken with the juices, which may need to be reduced by boiling in a pan, poured over as a sauce. Garnish with sesame seeds, chopped parsley and fine threads of orange zest (optional).

SERVES: 4

---◆---

CHICKEN PIRI PIRI

For this recipe it is best to use chicken joints with the skin on. The following amounts of spicy sauce can be doubled up if the recipe is to serve 4 people.

2 tablespoons olive oil
2 garlic cloves, crushed
1 tablespoon chopped fresh rosemary
1 or 2 teaspoons chilli powder
2 chicken joints

1 Mix the olive oil, garlic, rosemary and chilli powder together, and then pour over the chicken to coat the joints well.

2 Leave to marinate for half at least 30 minutes in the refrigerator.

3 Barbecue, basting the chicken pieces from time to time, until they are cooked. Alternatively, bake in a preheated oven at 200°C, 400°F, Gas Mark 6 for 30 minutes, basting with the spicy juices until the chicken is thoroughly cooked.

SERVES: 2

---◆---

JAMAICAN JERK CHICKEN

4 spring onions, trimmed and chopped
1-2 red or green chillies, seeded and chopped
50g/2oz allspice berries
salt and freshly ground black pepper
4 chicken joints

PEANUT SAUCE

1 tablespoon vegetable oil
115g/4oz unsalted peanuts
1 garlic clove, crushed
300ml/¹/₂ pint boiling water
115g/4oz creamed coconut, grated
juice of ¹/₂ lime or lemon
2 teaspoons light soy sauce
¹/₂ teaspoon ground cumin
¹/₂ teaspoon ground coriander
pinch of chilli powder

1 Heat the oil and sauté the peanuts for 3-4 minutes, until golden brown. Remove and cool. Fry the garlic in the oil for 1 minute, then process with the peanuts to a smooth paste in a food processor.

2 Pour the boiling water over the coconut and let it stand for 15 minutes. Strain the coconut milk into a saucepan and stir in the peanut paste and the remaining ingredients. Bring to the boil, stirring until the sauce thickens, then simmer for 5 minutes.

1 Pound the spring onions and chillies to a paste with the allspice berries and salt and pepper, either in a pestle and mortar, or in a food processor with the metal blade fitted.

2 Spread the paste over both sides of each chicken joint to flavour it – if it is too dry to spread, add a tiny amount of oil. Try to do this at least 30 minutes before cooking the chicken, to allow the flavour to penetrate.

3 Traditionally, the chicken is then barbecued, but it can also be placed under a preheated hot grill, and then grilled on each side until cooked through. Serve in the West Indian style with plain boiled rice, fried bananas or plantains, and some spicy hot pepper sauce.

SERVES: 4

EASTERN DISHES

Now that Thai and Indonesian ingredients are readily available in supermarkets as well as delicatessens and specialist stores, you can experiment with some new exotic dishes.

INDONESIAN VEGETABLE STEW (SAYUR LODEH)

2 tablespoons ground nut oil
1 large onion, chopped
1 garlic clove, chopped
2.5-cm/1-in piece fresh root ginger (or galangal),
peeled and chopped
1 small fresh green chilli, finely sliced
1 teaspoon trasi (dried shrimp paste)
3 teaspoons peanut butter
1 stick of lemon grass
1 x 200g/7oz can chopped tomatoes
1 x 400ml/14fl oz can coconut milk
300ml/1/2 pint vegetable or chicken stock
450g/1lb aubergines, preferably small thin ones,
cut into chunks
225g/8oz okra, trimmed
225g/8oz green beans, trimmed
1 1/2 teaspoons salt
1 teaspoon sugar

1 Heat the oil in a large pan, add the onion and stir over medium heat until it begins to brown.
2 Add the garlic, ginger (or galangal), chilli, trasi and peanut butter. Fry for 1 minute, crushing the trasi and the peanut butter with the back of a spoon so that there are no lumps.
3 Add the lemon grass and tomatoes, and cook for 3-4 minutes, then add the coconut milk and stock. Gently bring to the boil, stirring all the time, and then add all the vegetables, the salt and sugar.

4 Cook over low heat for just under 20 minutes, or until the vegetables are tender, stirring occasionally.
SERVES: 4

SPICY PRAWN SOUP (TOM YAM KAENG)

2 tablespoons vegetable oil
1 large onion, chopped
5-cm/2-in piece fresh root ginger,
peeled and chopped
3 garlic cloves, chopped
2 fresh green chillies, seeded and finely chopped
8 large uncooked prawns
900ml/1 1/2 pints fish or vegetable stock
2 teaspoons dried lemon grass
4 dried lime leaves
50g/2oz grated mooli (white radish)
1 teaspoon anchovy paste
50g/2oz creamed coconut, roughly chopped
few sprigs fresh coriander leaves, chopped

1 Heat the oil and add the onion, ginger and garlic. Stir-fry for 1 minute, then add the chillies with the prawns and continue stir-frying for 1-2 minutes.
2 Add the stock, lemon grass, mooli, anchovy paste and creamed coconut, and simmer gently for 10 minutes.
3 To serve, pour the soup into 4 bowls. Sprinkle with chopped coriander leaves.
SERVES: 4

Opposite: Spicy Prawn Soup

AROMATIC CRISPY DUCK

1 x 1.5kg/3¹/₄lb duck
4 teaspoons salt
1.8 litres/3 pints chicken stock
4 tablespoons dry sherry
175g/6oz sugar
9 pieces star anise
6 slices root ginger
1¹/₂ tablespoons Szechuan peppercorns
9 tablespoons light soy sauce
2 tablespoons dark soy sauce
1.2 litres/2 pints oil for deep frying
pancakes, shredded cucumber and spring onions, and
plum sauce, to serve

1 Cut the duck in half. Chop out the back bone and rib cage.
2 Heat all the ingredients, except the oil, in a wok. Add the duck halves and simmer for 1¹/₂-2 hours. Turn occasionally.
3 Remove the duck from the pan, drain and cool.
4 When ready to serve, heat the oil in a deep fat fryer until hot, and deep fry the duck until golden brown and crisp.
5 Drain on kitchen paper and shred at the table. Serve with pancakes, cucumber, spring onions and plum sauce.
SERVES: 2-3

PANCAKES

1 Mix 450g/1lb flour with 300ml/¹/₂ pint boiling water and a teaspoon of oil. Knead to a firm dough.
2 Divide into 3 pieces and roll out each one into a 'sausage' shape. Cut into 8 pieces and press each one out to a pancake with the palm of your hand.
3 Brush half of the pancakes with oil and press another one on top. Roll out in 15-cm/6-in circles.
4 Cook them in an ungreased frying pan, over medium heat, turning them when air bubbles appear on the surface. Remove and separate the 2 layers.

SWEET AND SOUR PRAWNS

2 tablespoons olive oil
1 garlic clove, chopped
10-cm/4-in piece cucumber, peeled and diced
1 x 227g/8oz can pineapple chunks, drained
175g/6oz prawns
225g/8oz tomatoes, skinned, seeded and chopped
1 tablespoon lemon juice
2-3 tablespoons oyster sauce
salt and pepper

1 Heat the olive oil in a wok and add the garlic. Stir-fry for 1 minute, then add the cucumber and pineapple.
2 Stir-fry for 1 minute, then add the prawns and tomatoes. Stir to heat through, and then finally add the lemon juice, oyster sauce and seasoning to taste.
3 Serve immediately with bruschetta (see page 34).
SERVES: 2

MOOLI RELISH

3 large carrots, grated
1-2 mooli, peeled and grated
¹/₂ teaspoon salt
1 teaspoon caster sugar
juice of 1 lemon
1 tablespoon oil
2 teaspoons black mustard seeds
1 teaspoon cumin seeds

1 Mix together the grated carrots and an equal quantity of mooli. Mix in the salt, sugar and lemon juice.
2 Heat the oil in a small pan and add the whole spices. Take care because they will splutter and spit.
3 After a few seconds, pour the oil with the seeds over the grated vegetables. Mix together and serve as a side dish with Thai food.

Opposite: Aromatic Crispy Duck

VEGETABLE BALTI

1kg/2¼lb mixed vegetables, e.g. potatoes, carrots,
broccoli, okra, courgettes, aubergines
4 tablespoons vegetable oil
2 garlic cloves, crushed
2.5-cm/1-in piece fresh root ginger, peeled and chopped
½ teaspoon chilli powder
4 small tomatoes, skinned and chopped
1 quantity Balti Sauce (see right)
1 x 420g/14oz can chick peas, drained
1 x 420g/14oz can yellow split peas, drained
1 tablespoon chopped fresh coriander
Balti Spice Mix (see below) or garam masala, to serve

1 Prepare the vegetables by peeling, cubing and par-boiling them until they are almost cooked. Drain well.

2 Heat the oil in a wok or Balti pan and stir-fry the garlic and ginger for a few seconds. Stir in the chilli powder, tomatoes and drained vegetables.
3 Add the Balti Sauce, chick peas and yellow split peas, and stir-fry quickly for 2-3 minutes, until the vegetables are thoroughly coated with the sauce and warmed through.
4 Serve sprinkled with coriander and Balti Spice Mix, with some naan bread or chapatis.
SERVES: 4

BALTI SPICE MIX

You can buy garam masala or Balti spice mix ready-made, but here is a recipe if you want to make your own.

1½ tablespoons black peppercorns
1 tablespoon cumin seeds
1½ teaspoons whole cloves
4 cardamon pods
5-cm/2-in cinnamon stick
½ whole nutmeg
3 star anise

Dry-roast all the spices until they are just beginning to brown. Bring together to a powder in a coffee grinder.
Note: This makes about 2½ tablespoons of spice mix, and can be stored out of sunlight in a screwtop jar.

BASIC BALTI SAUCE

3 tablespoons vegetable oil
1-cm/½-in piece fresh root ginger, peeled
and grated
2 garlic cloves, chopped
4 large onions, finely chopped
2 teaspoons ground coriander
1 teaspoon ground cumin
½ teaspoon chilli powder
½ teaspoon paprika
1 teaspoon garam masala
1½ teaspoons salt
2 bay leaves
3 cardamom pods
1½ teaspoons ground fenugreek
4 tomatoes, skinned and chopped
250ml/9fl oz water

1 Heat the oil in a large pan and stir-fry the ginger and garlic for a few seconds. Add the onions and fry until translucent and softened.
2 Add the coriander, cumin, chilli, paprika, garam masala, salt, bay leaves, cardamom and fenugreek. Stir-fry for 1 minute, then stir in the tomatoes and water.
3 Simmer, covered, for 20 minutes, then remove from the heat and discard the bay leaves and cardamom pods. Cool a little, then thoroughly blend or liquidize. The sauce can be poured into a screwtop jar and will keep for up to 1 week in the refrigerator.

LAMB WITH SPINACH (SAAG GOSHT)

4 tablespoons vegetable oil
4 cardamom pods
4 whole cloves
1 bay leaf
1 medium onion, finely chopped
4 garlic cloves, finely chopped
1 teaspoon finely chopped fresh root ginger
675g/1¹/₂lb lean lamb, cut into 2.5-cm/1-in cubes
2 level teaspoons ground cumin seeds
1 level teaspoon ground coriander seeds
¹/₂-1 teaspoon cayenne pepper
1¹/₂ teaspoons salt
4 tablespoons plain yogurt
675g/1¹/₂lb chopped spinach, fresh or frozen
freshly ground black pepper

1 Heat the oil in a large saucepan, and add the cardamom pods, cloves and bay leaf. Stir-fry briefly, then add the onion, garlic and ginger. Continue stir-frying until the onion begins to brown at the edges.
2 Add the lamb, ground cumin, coriander, cayenne pepper, ground black pepper and half of the salt, and cook, turning the lamb occasionally, until the meat is brown all over.
3 Add the yogurt, a tablespoon at a time, stirring and frying between each spoonful until all the yogurt has been incorporated.
4 Add the spinach and the remaining salt and stir to mix. If you are using fresh spinach, keep stirring until it wilts completely; if frozen, until the spinach has defrosted.
5 Cover the pan tightly and simmer for about 1 hour, or until the lamb is tender. Raise the heat and remove the lid for the last 5 minutes or so, until most of the liquid from the spinach disappears and you are left with a thick green sauce.
SERVES: 4

Below: Lamb with Spinach (Saag Gosht)

NICK DAY

Before becoming a successful actor with a career embracing the theatre and television, Nick Day worked as a commis chef. He has appeared several times on *This Morning*, demonstrating his style of quick, simple cookery that does not compromise on taste.

GREEN CHICKEN CURRY

1 x 400ml/14fl oz can coconut milk
4 tablespoons Green Curry Paste
4 chicken breast fillets, cut into chunks
2 tablespoons Thai fish sauce
small handful of citrus (kaffir) leaves
2 long thin green chillies
handful of fresh basil leaves
fresh coriander sprigs, to garnish
salt, to taste

1 Open the can of coconut milk and dig through the thick coconut paste if it has collected at one end, and empty the thin watery milk into a bowl. Scrape the thickened part out into a pan or wok.
2 Add the Green Curry Paste and cook gently for 5 minutes, stirring frequently.
3 Add the chicken and cook for 5 minutes, still stirring. Add the reserved thinner coconut milk, fish sauce and the citrus leaves, and continue cooking for 15 minutes.
4 Meanwhile, remove the seeds from one of the chillies by splitting it in half and scraping them out with a teaspoon. Remove the stem ends from both chillies and chop finely with the basil leaves. Take care not to rub your eyes after de-seeding the chillies – wash your hands straight away.
5 Stir the chillies and basil into the curry, and then cook for 5 minutes. Salt to taste. Serve garnished with coriander leaves with plain boiled rice.
SERVES: 4

GREEN CURRY PASTE

4 long thin fresh green chillies
2 teaspoons ground coriander
1 teaspoon black peppercorns
1 teaspoon ground cumin
1 small onion, quartered
1 teaspoon shrimp paste
3 garlic cloves, peeled
1 teaspoon turmeric
2 teaspoons lemon rind
1 tablespoon groundnut oil
handful of fresh coriander sprigs
4 tablespoons water
1 teaspoon salt
1 teaspoon ground galangal (or 1-cm/^{1}/$_2$-in piece
fresh root ginger, peeled and chopped)

1 Cut the stem ends off the chillies and scoop the seeds out of three of them.
2 Blend the chillies with all the remaining ingredients in a blender or food processor, pushing and scraping it all down with a spatula as necessary, and adding a little more water if it is too stiff.

NOTE ON THAI COOKING

Thai food is often uncompromisingly hot. I have tried to make these recipes a little milder than you might encounter in a Thai restaurant. However you can add more chillies, if wished.

SPRING ROLLS WITH A DIPPING SAUCE

*2.5-cm/1-in piece fresh root ginger,
peeled and chopped
1 tablespoon oil
2 carrots, grated
2 onions, finely chopped
375g/12oz bean sprouts
2 teaspoons dark soy sauce
375g/12oz filo pastry
oil for brushing
salt and pepper*

FOR THE DIPPING SAUCE:
*2 large red peppers, seeded and cut
into chunks
4 garlic cloves, peeled
water, to cover
dash of Tabasco or hot chilli sauce
salt and pepper*

FOR THE SPRING ONION TASSELS:
small bunch of spring onions

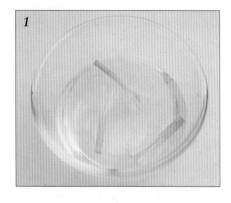

1 Trim the spring onions to about 12.5cm/5in, cutting off the root. Rinse in cold water and then make a series of cuts with a sharp knife through the green top end of each onion, to make a tassel. Place in a bowl of iced water and set aside for at least 1 hour, until they curl open.

2 Make the sauce. Put the peppers and garlic in a small saucepan with just enough water to cover them. Simmer for 10 minutes, then drain. Purée the peppers and garlic in a blender or processor, and season with salt and pepper and a dash of Tabasco or chilli sauce. Only add water if the sauce seems too thick. Set aside to cool.

3 Prepare the filling for the spring rolls. Fry the ginger in the oil for 1 minute in a wok or frying pan. Add the carrots and onions, and stir-fry. Add the bean sprouts and stir-fry for 30 seconds. Season with salt and pepper and soy sauce.

4 Cut through the sheets of filo pastry to make 17.5-cm/7-in squares. Taking one square at a time, put a spoonful of the filling near one corner of the square. Fold the corner over the filling, tuck in the sides, and roll up towards the far corner. Place the spring rolls on an oiled baking sheet and brush them with oil. Bake in a preheated oven at 200°C, 400°F, Gas Mark 6 for 20 minutes, turning them over halfway through. Serve with the dipping sauce and spring onion tassels.
SERVES: 4-6

Vincent Osborne is a pioneer of Caribbean cooking, or 'Cuisine Antillaise' through his Brixtonian restaurant in London. His food is influenced by the different styles of the islands, e.g. French Martinique, Dutch Aruba and Spanish Curaçao.

SNAPPER WITH CALALOO

1 x 1.3kg/3lb red snapper
2 garlic cloves, crushed
juice of 1 lime
1 tablespoon chopped fresh root ginger
115ml/4fl oz dry white wine
2 bay leaves
few sprigs of thyme and tarragon
2 plantain, peeled and sliced diagonally
1 tablespoon oil
15g/¹/₂oz butter
salt and pepper

FOR THE CALALOO:
450g/1lb calaloo or spinach
50g/2oz butter
2 tablespoons olive oil
2 garlic cloves, crushed
1 tablespoon chopped fresh root ginger
15g/¹/₂oz brown sugar
50g/2oz sultanas
50ml/2fl oz rum
50g/2oz pine kernels
salt and pepper

1 Season the red snapper with salt, pepper, garlic, lime juice and ginger. Transfer to a shallow pan of gently boiling water, pre-seasoned with the white wine and herbs. Cover and cook for 20 minutes.
2 Fry the plantain in the oil and butter until golden.
3 Blanch the calaloo (if using) in hot water and drain well. Sauté the calaloo or spinach in the butter and olive oil with the garlic and ginger.
4 Add the brown sugar, sultanas soaked in rum and pine kernels. Stir-fry gently for 2 minutes and season to taste. Serve on a platter with the red snapper.
SERVES: 3-4

MANGO CHOW

6 mangoes, stoned and peeled
4 ruby grapefruits, peeled and segmented
oak leaf lettuce leaves, to garnish

FOR THE MARINADE:
juice and zest of 2 limes
6 Scotch bonnet peppers, finely chopped
2 cloves garlic
2 bay leaves
few sprigs of thyme
115ml/4fl oz dry white wine
2 tablespoons chopped fresh coriander
2 tablespoons chopped fresh parsley

1 Cut the mango flesh into strips. Mix the marinade and add the mango and grapefruit. Leave for 1 hour.
2 To serve, arrange the mango strips and grapefruit segments on a bed of lettuce leaves.
SERVES: 4

Opposite: Snapper with Calaloo

CHAPTER SEVEN

ENTERTAINING

◆

Entertaining couldn't be easier if you choose
a menu from this chapter. There are menus
for every occasion, from quiet family get-
togethers to more sophisticated dinner parties.
The secret of successful entertaining lies in
the preparation and presentation, so plan
ahead and leave yourself plenty of time to
shop and cook. If possible, choose dishes
that you can prepare in advance.

Salmon en Croûte with a Spinach Filling (see page 100)

Menu

SERVES 4

Leek and Potato Soup

Salmon en Croûte with a
Spinach Filling

Strawberry and Passion
Fruit Pavlova

LEEK AND
POTATO SOUP

2 large leeks, washed, trimmed and thinly sliced
1 large onion, thinly sliced
25g/1oz butter
225g/8oz potatoes, cut into small dice
1.2 litres/2 pints chicken stock
115ml/4fl oz double cream
2 tablespoons chopped fresh chives
salt and freshly ground black pepper
bread croûtons, to serve

1 Sweat the leeks and onion in the butter with the potatoes. Do not allow them to colour.
2 Add the chicken stock and bring to the boil. Reduce the heat and simmer for 20 minutes, skimming the surface occasionally. Season to taste and liquidize until smooth.
3 Stir in the double cream and pour into bowls. Scatter with bread croûtons and serve.

SALMON EN CROUTE
WITH A SPINACH FILLING

225g/8oz spinach, washed and trimmed
75ml/3fl oz double cream
350g/12oz puff pastry
1 egg, beaten
2 tablespoons semolina
1.3kg/3lb salmon, skinned, boned and filleted
25g/1oz butter
2 shallots, chopped
small bunch chives, chopped
2 tablespoons white wine vinegar
1/2 glass dry white wine
300ml/1/2 pint fish stock
pinch of cayenne pepper
salt and freshly ground black pepper

1 Blanch the spinach in boiling water. Drain, pressing down well in a colander with a saucer, season and chop. Mix the spinach with 25ml/1fl oz of the double cream.
2 Roll out the puff pastry thinly into a rectangle. Make an incision at each corner ready to fold the pastry. Brush with beaten egg and sprinkle with semolina, leaving a 2.5-cm/1-in border.
3 Lay one piece of salmon on top of the pastry and pile the spinach on top. Cover with the second salmon fillet.
4 Fold over the puff pastry to make a parcel and seal. Turn the pastry parcel over so that the joins are now underneath. Leave to relax for 1 hour in the refrigerator.
5 Brush with beaten egg and cut a small hole in the top of the pastry. Decorate with any pastry trimmings.
6 Place on a greased baking sheet and cook in a preheated oven for at 230°C, 450°F, Gas Mark 8. After 10 minutes, reduce the oven temperature to 180°C, 350°F, Gas Mark 4, and bake for a further 20 minutes until well-risen and golden brown.
7 Meanwhile, make the sauce. Melt the butter and sweat the shallots and chives without colouring.
8 Add the wine vinegar, wine and fish stock and boil to reduce to a syrup. Add the remaining cream and boil to a sauce consistency. Season to taste with cayenne pepper and salt.

9 Allow the cooked salmon parcel to rest for 10 minutes, then pour a little sauce through the hole in the top of the pastry. Cut the Salmon en Croûte in slices and serve the remaining sauce separately.

STRAWBERRY AND PASSION FRUIT PAVLOVA

300ml/¹/2 pint whipping cream
50g/2oz caster sugar
2 passion fruit
175g/6oz strawberries, hulled and sliced
icing sugar, for dusting
25g/1oz toasted flaked almonds

FOR THE MERINGUE:
3 egg whites
175g/6oz caster sugar
1 teaspoon cornflour
1 teaspoon vinegar

1 Make the meringue. Whisk the egg whites until stiff, then gradually whisk in the sugar, a little at a time, until stiff and silky.
2 Mix in the cornflour and vinegar, and pipe or pile on to a baking sheet lined with baking parchment. Make a large circle of meringue and hollow out the centre slightly.
3 Bake in a preheated oven at 130°C, 250°F, Gas Mark ¹/2, for 1¹/4 to 1¹/2 hours. Remove from the oven and set aside to cool.
4 Whisk the cream and sugar until semi-stiff. Scoop out the pulp from the passion fruit and mix into the cream.
5 Mix in the strawberries and pile into the pavlova. Dust with icing sugar and sprinkle with toasted almonds.

A N T O N Y
W O R R A L L
T H O M P S O N

Antony Worrall Thompson is well known for his frequent appearances on television and radio. He has opened several restaurants in London, including Menage à Trois, and in 1988 he received the prestigious award of Meilleur Ouvrier de Grande Bretagne – the chef's Oscar, awarded by the Académie Culinaire.

SCALLOPS WITH GREEN MANGO

6 raw diver scallops, thinly sliced horizontally
2 tablespoons clear honey
2 tablespoons nam pla (fish sauce)
2 tablespoons lime juice
2 green mangoes, peeled, stoned and finely diced
(if unavailable, use tart green apples)
2 tomatoes, skinned, seeded and finely diced
1 bunch spring onions, finely sliced
2 tablespoons finely chopped fresh coriander
2 tablespoons finely chopped lemon grass
1 teaspoon finely chopped garlic
1 teaspoon finely chopped red chilli
sprigs of coriander, to garnish

1 Arrange the scallop slices on 4 chilled serving plates.
2 Combine all the remaining ingredients and divide between the 4 plates. Serve immediately, garnished with coriander leaves.

Menu

SERVES *4*

Scallops with Green Mango

Lemon and Tarragon Chicken

Melon and Ginger Ice Cream

LEMON AND TARRAGON CHICKEN

2 tablespoons olive oil
1 red pepper, deseeded and sliced
1 green pepper, deseeded and sliced
1 x 227g/8oz can water chestnuts, drained and sliced
115g/4oz bean sprouts
4 cooked chicken breasts, skinned and sliced
4 spring onions, trimmed and shredded
450g/1lb egg noodles or pasta
salt and freshly ground black pepper

FOR THE DRESSING:
1 teaspoon clear honey
grated zest of 1/2 lemon
1 teaspoon chopped fresh tarragon
2 tablespoons grape or apple juice
2 tablespoons tarragon vinegar
1 teaspoon sesame oil

1 Heat the olive oil in a wok or deep frying pan and stir-fry the red and green peppers for 2 minutes. Add the water chestnuts, bean sprouts and chicken, and stir-fry for 1 minute.

2 Add the spring onions and heat through. Season to taste with salt and pepper.

3 Meanwhile, cook the noodles or pasta in boiling lightly salted water, according to the packet instructions, until tender. Drain well.

4 Mix all the ingredients for the dressing and use to toss the hot noodles. Serve immediately with the stir-fried chicken mixture.

MELON AND GINGER ICE CREAM

6 egg yolks
50g/2oz sugar
115ml/4fl oz water
6 tablespoons green ginger wine
300ml/¹/₂ pint double cream, whipped
175g/6oz melon, cubed
4 pieces preserved ginger in syrup, thinly sliced
melon balls and sliced preserved ginger, to decorate

1 Whisk the egg yolks in a bowl until light and fluffy. Dissolve the sugar in the water, stirring over medium heat. Pour this liquid in a steady stream over the yolks, whisking vigorously until cool. It should resemble thick whipped cream.

2 Whisk in the ginger wine and fold in the whipped double cream, melon and ginger. Pour into a freezing tray and freeze for at least 8 hours.

3 Remove from the freezer about 10 minutes before serving. Serve in individual glasses decorated with melon balls and ginger.

Opposite: Lemon and Tarragon Chicken

Menu

SERVES 4

*Salad of Mushrooms
in Red Wine*

*Pan Fried Steaks with
Victoria Plums*

Lemon Pudding

SALAD OF MUSHROOMS
IN RED WINE

6 rashers smoked bacon, diced
3 tablespoons olive oil
2 garlic cloves, crushed
225g/8oz dark mushrooms, sliced
200ml/7fl oz red wine
2 tablespoons chopped fresh parsley
8 slices French bread
50g/2oz melted butter
salad leaves, to garnish
salt and freshly ground black pepper

1 Fry the diced bacon in the olive oil until golden brown, then add the garlic. Add the mushrooms and sauté briskly.
2 Add the wine and set light to the mixture. When the flames die down, bring to the boil and reduce the liquid. Season to taste and add the chopped parsley.
3 Dip the French bread in melted butter and bake in a

preheated oven at 180°C, 350°F, Gas Mark 4 for about 10 minutes, until crisp and golden. Pile the mushroom mixture on top and serve, garnished with salad leaves.

PAN FRIED STEAKS
WITH VICTORIA PLUMS

4 x 150g/5oz steaks
1 glass red wine
1 tablespoon red wine vinegar
2 tablespoons redcurrant jelly
2 tablespoons oil
225g/8oz Victoria plums
50g/2oz butter
1 teaspoon Dijon mustard
salt and freshly ground black pepper

FOR THE MARINADE:
1 tablespoon clear honey
1 tablespoon dark soy sauce
juice of 1 lemon
1 tablespoon olive oil
1 teaspoon grated fresh root ginger
2 garlic cloves, crushed

1 Mix all the marinade ingredients together in a bowl. Season the steaks with salt and pepper. and then add to the marinade. Leave in a cool place for 1 hour.
2 Remove the steaks and pat dry with kitchen paper. Strain the marinade into a pan, and add the wine, vinegar and redcurrant jelly. Boil to reduce by half.
3 Heat the oil in a frying pan and sauté the steaks, as required. Remove from the pan and keep warm.
4 Stone and quarter the plums, and quickly sauté them in the hot oil in the frying pan. Add the reduced marinade, cook for 2-3 minutes and then stir in the butter.
5 Remove from the heat and stir in the mustard. Pour over the steaks and serve immediately with new potatoes and a green salad.

LEMON PUDDING

75g/3oz butter, softened
225g/8oz caster sugar
grated zest and juice of 3 lemons
50g/2oz plain flour, sifted
5 large eggs, separated
300ml/¹/₂ pint milk
crème fraîche and raspberries, redcurrants and
strawberries, to serve

1 Beat the butter and sugar together in a bowl until pale and fluffy. Beat in the lemon zest and juice with a teaspoon of the flour to prevent it curdling.

2 Beat the egg yolks into the mixture, then add spoonfuls of flour alternately with the milk.

3 Whisk the egg whites until stiff and fold into the lemon mixture.

4 Pour into a well-buttered large soufflé dish and stand in a roasting pan filled with 5cm/2in water.

5 Bake in a preheated oven at 180°C, 350°F, Gas Mark 4 for 50 minutes, until set and golden brown.

6 Serve hot or cold with crème fraîche and red berry fruits.

Below: Salad of Mushrooms in Red Wine

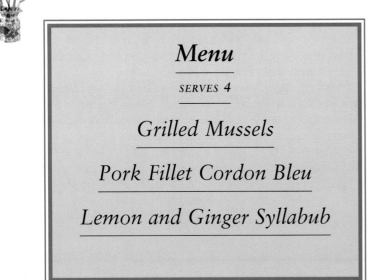

Menu

SERVES 4

Grilled Mussels

Pork Fillet Cordon Bleu

Lemon and Ginger Syllabub

GRILLED MUSSELS

40 plump live mussels
1 glass dry white wine
175g/6oz butter
2 tablespoons chopped fresh parsley
1 garlic clove, crushed
1 shallot, finely chopped
good pinch of ground nutmeg
50g/2oz white breadcrumbs
freshly ground black pepper

1 Wash and scrub the mussels under cold running water and put into a colander to drain well. Place them in a large saucepan with the white wine. Cover with a lid and cook over high heat until the mussels open, shaking occasionally.
2 Remove the mussels with a slotted spoon and set aside to cool. Throw away any mussels that do not open.
3 Boil up the cooking liquor to reduce by half, then strain again into a bowl and add the butter, parsley, garlic, shallot, nutmeg and pepper. Work into a smooth paste.
4 Take one half of each shell off the mussels, leaving the mussels in their half-shells. Divide them between 4 gratin

dishes — 10 per portion. Put a small amount of the paste on each mussel and sprinkle with breadcrumbs.
5 Bake under a preheated hot grill until crisp and golden. Serve immediately with French bread.

◆

PORK FILLET CORDON BLEU

8 slices pork fillet, approx. 2.5 cm/1 in thick
4 slices ham
4 slices Bel Paese cheese
2 tablespoons flour
75g/3oz butter
115ml/4fl oz port
115g/4oz fromage frais
1 teaspoon chopped fresh rosemary
salt and freshly ground black pepper

1 Beat each slice of pork fillet to a thin escalope between 2 sheets of greaseproof paper.
2 Place a slice of ham and one of cheese on top of 4 of the escalopes, and cover with the remaining escalopes.
3 Seal the ham and cheese inside by pressing the edges of the escalopes together (dab a little flour first around the edges to seal).
4 Season the flour with salt and pepper and use to lightly coat the escalopes. Fry in butter until golden brown on both sides. Remove from the pan and keep warm.
5 Add the port to the pan juices and bring to the boil. Boil until reduced by half, then whisk in the fromage frais and heat through.
6 Add the chopped rosemary and season to taste. Serve the sauce with the escalopes.

Variation: this dish is equally delicious if you use chicken breasts instead. Fill with sage leaves and slices of mozzarella cheese and then sandwich together and wrap in thin slices of Parma ham. Fry as above, adding Marsala instead of Madeira.

ENTERTAINING

LEMON AND
GINGER SYLLABUB

115g/4oz ginger biscuits
300ml/¹/₂ pint double cream
grated zest and juice of 1 lemon
115g/4oz caster sugar
4 tablespoons sherry or brandy

1 Crush the biscuits to crumbs in a food processor, or put

them in a polythene bag and hit them with a rolling pin.
2 Put the cream, lemon zest and juice, sugar and sherry or brandy in a bowl. Whisk until thick and floppy, and it just holds its shape.
3 Take 4 long-stemmed glasses and put a spoonful of cream mixture in the bottom of each glass, then sprinkle with ginger crumbs. Continue layering the cream and crumbs in this way, finishing with a sprinkling of crumbs. Chill well before serving.

Below: Pork Fillet Cordon Bleu

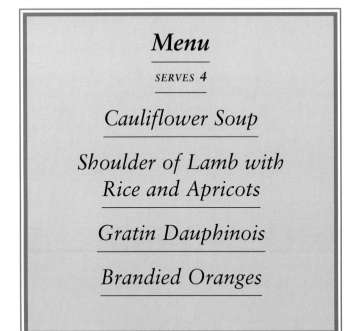

Menu

SERVES 4

Cauliflower Soup

Shoulder of Lamb with Rice and Apricots

Gratin Dauphinois

Brandied Oranges

CAULIFLOWER SOUP

1.2 litres/2 pints chicken stock
1 cauliflower, trimmed and divided into florets, stalk
reserved
75g/3oz butter
115g/4oz white of leek, chopped
50g/2oz finely chopped onion
1 potato, peeled and chopped
50g/2oz flour
2 tablespoons chopped fresh parsley
300ml/¹/₂ pint double cream
1 egg yolk
salt and freshly ground black pepper

1 Bring the chicken stock to the boil in a large saucepan. Add the cauliflower florets and cook until tender. Remove and refresh, reserving the stock.
2 In another pan, melt 50g/2oz of the butter and add the leek, onion and the reserved cauliflower stalk. Cook

gently until softened, without colouring. Add the potato and soften.
3 Mix with the flour, then gradually add the reserved chicken stock and bring to the boil.
4 Cook gently for 15 minutes and then purée in a blender or food processor. Return to the pan and bring back to the boil.
5 Sauté the cauliflower florets in the remaining butter until golden. Add the parsley.
6 Mix the cream with the egg yolk. Add the hot soup, stirring well, then return to the pan. Reheat without boiling and season to taste. Pour into serving bowls and sprinkle the cauliflower florets on top.

SHOULDER OF LAMB WITH RICE AND APRICOTS

175g/6oz long-grain rice
50g/2oz dried apricots, soaked and chopped
25g/1oz seedless raisins
25g/1oz flaked almonds
pinch of ground cinnamon
2 tablespoons chopped fresh coriander
1 x 2kg/4¹/₂lb boned shoulder of lamb
salt and pepper
oil for roasting

1 Boil the rice in lightly salted water until tender. Drain well and mix with apricots, raisins, almonds, cinnamon and coriander. Season with salt and pepper.
2 Fill the pocket in the boned shoulder of lamb with the rice stuffing, reserving any excess rice, and then sew up securely. Tie with string to help it keep its shape during cooking.
3 Roast in a preheated oven at 200°C, 400°F, Gas Mark 6, for about 1¹/₂ hours. Remove from the oven and rest for 10 minutes before removing the string.
4 Carve the lamb and then serve on a bed of the reserved rice.

GRATIN DAUPHINOIS

1 garlic clove, peeled
75g/3oz butter, softened
1kg/2lb waxy potatoes, peeled and sliced thinly
freshly grated nutmeg
350ml/12fl oz hot milk
250ml/9fl oz single cream
salt and freshly ground black pepper

1 Rub the garlic clove round the inside of an ovenproof dish, then brush thicky with some of the butter.
2 Arrange the potatoes in a layer in the dish. Sprinkle with nutmeg, salt and pepper, then continue layering up in this way until they are all used.
3 Mix the hot milk and cream and pour over the potatoes. Dot the top with the remaining butter and bake in a preheated oven at 180°C, 350°F, Gas Mark 4 for 1-1 1/4 hours. Increase the temperature to 200°C, 400°F, Gas Mark 6 for the last 10 minutes to brown the top.

BRANDIED ORANGES

8 small oranges
3 tablespoons brandy
1 tablespoon crushed sugar
1 tablespoon grenadine
clotted cream or crème fraîche, to serve

1 Using a zester, remove the zest from the oranges in long, thin, curly strips. Blanch the orange zest in a small saucepan of boiling water, drain and refresh.
2 Peel the oranges and cut away the pith. Cut out the segments and place in a bowl with the excess juice. Add the brandy and sugar, and leave in a cool place for 3 hours.
3 Bring the grenadine to the boil and add the orange zest. Bring back to the boil, then reduce the heat and simmer until all the liquid has evaporated. Leave to cool, then pour over the oranges.
4 Serve the oranges in a dish with the juice, decorated with the orange zest. Serve with clotted cream or crème fraîche.

Menu

SERVES 4

Arbroath Smokie Pâté

---

*Roast Pheasant with
Wild Mushrooms*

Tarte Citron

ARBROATH SMOKIE PATE

*pair of Arbroath smokies, boned and skinned
juice of 1/2 lemon
pinch of cayenne pepper
225g/8oz cream cheese
150ml/1/4 pint double cream
salt and freshly ground black pepper, to taste
buttered toast, to serve*

1 Liquidize the Arbroath smokies, lemon juice and cayenne pepper.
2 Place in a bowl, add the cream cheese and mix with a

DELICIOUS FISH PATES

Instead of using Arbroath smokies, try using smoked salmon or trout, or kippers.

wooden spoon until smooth. Add the cream and mix well. Season to taste.
3 Spoon the pâté into 4 small ramekin dishes and chill in the refrigerator until required. Serve with hot fingers of buttered toast.

ROAST PHEASANT WITH WILD MUSHROOMS

*2 young oven-ready hen pheasants
115g/4oz unsalted butter
12 juniper berries
4 rashers streaky bacon
600ml/1 pint game stock
450g/1lb celeriac, peeled and diced
3 tablespoons olive oil
8oz/250g wild mushrooms, e.g. chanterelles, blewits, chopped
salt and freshly ground black pepper*

1 Insert a knob of butter and 3 juniper berries in the body cavity of each pheasant. Place 2 bacon rashers over each breast and then truss the birds.
2 Place the pheasants on their side in a roasting pan. Roast in the centre of a preheated oven at 230°C/450°F/Gas Mark 8. After 8-10 minutes, turn the pheasants over and cook on the other side for 8-10 minutes (this time may vary slightly depending on the size of the bird). Remove from the oven and set aside to rest.
3 Boil up the game stock and reduce by one-third. Whisk in the remaining butter, season to taste and set aside until required.
4 Meanwhile, cook the celeriac in the olive oil over medium heat for 5 minutes, then add the mushrooms and continue cooking for a further 3 minutes, stirring occasionally. Season to taste.
5 Joint the pheasants by removing the legs and breasts. Spoon the celeriac and mushrooms on to the centre of each warm serving plate. Place a pheasant breast and leg on top and spoon over the sauce. Serve immediately.

TARTE CITRON

1 x 20-cm/8-in pastry shortcrust or
sweet pastry flan case
6 eggs
250g/9oz caster sugar
grated zest of 2 lemons
200ml/8fl oz double cream
juice of 4 lemons

1 Whisk the eggs, sugar and lemon zest together in a large bowl. Add the double cream and lemon juice, and leave to stand for 1 hour, until the foam settles on top. Skim off the foam.

2 Meanwhile, fill the uncooked pastry flan case with foil and baking beans, and 'bake blind' in a preheated oven at 200°C, 400°F, Gas Mark 6 for 10-15 minutes. Remove the baking beans and foil.

3 Pour the lemon filling into the warm pastry case and bake in the preheated oven. After 5 minutes, lower the oven temperature to 150°C, 300°F, Gas Mark 2 and continue cooking for 25-30 minutes, or until set. Serve warm, cut into slices, with cream.

Below: Tarte Citron

Menu

SERVES 4

Goat's Cheese Darioles
(see page 72)

Skate with Black Butter Sauce

Petits Pots au Chocolate
(see page 126)

COURT BOUILLON

300ml/¹/₂ pint dry cider
1.2 litres/2 pints water
75ml/3fl oz white wine vinegar
1 onion, roughly chopped
2 carrots, roughly chopped
2 celery sticks, roughly chopped
2 fresh or dried bay leaves
1 teaspoon salt
12 peppercorns

1 Bring all the court-bouillon ingredients to the boil in a large saucepan.
2 Remove the pan of court bouillon from the heat and then leave to cool before using, to complete the infusion of flavours.

Note: court bouillon can be used as the base for many sauces to be served with fish, as well as for cooking a whole salmon or salmon trout. You can double the quantity and freeze half for later use.

RICK
STEIN

Rick Stein runs The Seafood Restaurant in Padstow, Cornwall, with his wife Jill. He graduated in English from Oxford University before opening the restaurant in 1975. His book *English Seafood Cookery* won the 1989 Glenfiddich Award for Food Book of the Year. He has also presented a successful fish cookery series on BBC television.

SKATE WITH BLACK BUTTER

900g/2lb skate wings
1 quantity court bouillon (see left)
15g/¹/₂oz capers

FOR THE BLACK BUTTER:
175g/6oz salted butter
50ml/2fl oz red wine vinegar
1 tablespoon finely chopped parsley

1 Cut the skate into 4 portions and place in a wide shallow pan. Pour the court bouillon over the fish, bring to the boil and then simmer very gently for 15-20 minutes, depending on the thickness of the skate. Drain the fish and keep it warm on a serving dish. Sprinkle with the capers.
2 Make the black butter. Melt the butter in a frying pan, and when it foams, starts to turn dark and smell nutty, pour in the vinegar.
3 Add the parsley, boil for a few minutes to reduce, and then pour over the skate. Serve immediately with plain boiled potatoes.

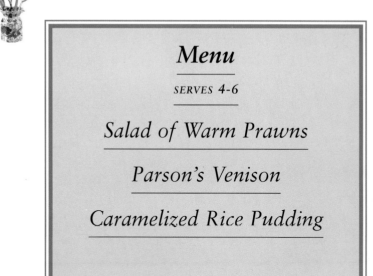

Menu

SERVES *4-6*

Salad of Warm Prawns

Parson's Venison

Caramelized Rice Pudding

SALAD OF WARM PRAWNS

1/2 small red chilli, deseeded
1/2 small green chilli, deseeded
2 spring onions, trimmed
4 tomatoes, skinned and deseeded
1 garlic clove, crushed
2 tablespoons groundnut oil
1 teaspoon rice vinegar
1/2 tablespoon soy sauce
1 tablespoon sesame oil
450g/1lb peeled prawns
fine sea salt, to season
3 tablespoons chopped fresh parsley
25g/1oz butter
selection of salad leaves

1 Put the chillies, red pepper, spring onions and tomatoes in a blender and process until smooth. Add the garlic, groundnut oil, vinegar, soy sauce and sesame oil. Season to taste with salt and chill until needed.
2 Rinse the prawns in 2 tablespoons of iced water and drain well. Season with fine sea salt and chopped parsley and leave in the refrigerator for at least 30 minutes.

3 Melt the butter, add the prawns and sauté lightly. Mix into the sauce. Arrange the salad leaves on 4 serving plates and top with the prawns.

PARSON'S VENISON

25g/1oz butter
1 shallot, finely chopped
115g/4oz mushrooms, chopped
115g/4oz cooked ham, chopped
2 tablespoons chopped fresh chives
1 x 2.2kg/5lb leg of lamb, boned
300ml/1/2 pint red wine
150ml/1/4 pint port
6 crushed juniper berries
1/4 teaspoon ground allspice
3 tablespoons red wine vinegar
1 bay leaf
1/4 teaspoon grated nutmeg
olive oil for roasting
salt and freshly ground black pepper

1 Melt the butter, add the shallot and mushrooms and cook until softened. Add the ham and chives, season with salt and pepper and leave to cool.
2 Stuff the lamb with the mushroom and ham mixture, and tie with string.
3 Mix together the red wine, port, juniper berries, allspice, vinegar, bay leaf and nutmeg, and pour this marinade over the lamb in a suitable container. Leave to marinate for 24 hours, turning and basting the lamb frequently.
4 Remove the lamb from the marinade and dry well. Heat the oil in a large flameproof casserole dish and brown the lamb on all sides. Pour the marinade over the lamb and bring to the boil.
5 Cover and cook in a preheated oven at 180°C, 350°F, Gas Mark 4, for 2 hours, basting occasionally, until tender.
6 Remove the lamb and keep warm. Boil the cooking liquor until reduced. Serve the lamb carved into slices accompanied by the sauce.

CARAMELIZED RICE PUDDING

115g/4oz short-grain pudding rice
1 litre/1³/₄ pints milk
115g/4oz caster sugar
4 eggs
2-3 drops vanilla essence
115g/4oz fruit, e.g. strawberries, cherries, raspberries
Demerara sugar, for sprinkling

1 Put the rice and milk in a saucepan and bring to the boil, stirring constantly. Simmer for 30 minutes, or until tender.
2 Whisk together the sugar, eggs and vanilla, then gradually stir into the rice. Heat through gently until the rice gets thick and creamy. Set aside to cool.
3 Arrange the fruit in 4 individual ovenproof dishes or one large dish. Cover with the cold rice pudding, and then sprinkle with Demerara sugar.
4 Place under a preheated hot grill until the sugar melts and caramelizes. Chill in the refrigerator before serving.

Below: Caramelized Rice Pudding

CHAPTER EIGHT

DESSERTS AND PUDDINGS

◆

There are all kinds of delicious desserts in this chapter, including many comforting winter pies and puddings, sumptous recipes for special occasions, and refreshing fruit mousses, soufflés and fools. For chocaholics there are some wicked Petits Pots au Chocolat and heavenly Dark Chocolate Tartlets. All your old favourites are also featured including Sticky Toffee Pudding and Jam Roly Poly.

Bread and Butter Pudding (see page 119)

STICKY TOFFEE PUDDING

225g/8oz dates, stoned and chopped
150ml/¹/₄ pint water
¹/₂ teaspoon bicarbonate of soda
25g/1oz butter, softened
75g/3oz caster sugar
1 egg, beaten
115g/4oz plain flour
¹/₂ teaspoon baking powder
¹/₂ teaspoon vanilla essence
oil for greasing
whipped or clotted cream, to serve

FOR THE SAUCE:
100g/3¹/₂oz soft dark brown sugar
50ml/2fl oz single cream
50g/2oz butter
1-2 drops vanilla essence

1 Put the dates and water in a small saucepan and bring to the boil. Add the bicarbonate of soda and stir well.

Remove the pan from the heat and set aside to cool.
2 Beat the butter and sugar together until pale and fluffy. Add the beaten egg gradually, beating all the time.
3 Sift the flour and baking powder together, and fold half into the creamed mixture with a metal spoon. Gradually fold in the remainder.
4 Stir in the date mixture and a few drops of vanilla essence, then pour the mixture into 6 individual oiled 7.5-cm/3-in pudding moulds. Leave about 2.5cm/1in spare below each rim. The mixture will be quite runny.
5 Bake in a preheated oven at 180°C, 350°F, Gas Mark 4 for about 20-30 minutes, until the sponges are springy to the touch and an inserted skewer comes out clean.
6 Turn out the puddings on to a wire cooling rack.
7 Put all the ingredients for the sauce into a saucepan and heat gently. Bring to the boil, stirring all the time, then boil for 2 minutes, until thick. Remove from the heat.
8 Place each pudding on a warm plate, pour the sauce over the top and serve with cream.
SERVES: 6

RHUBARB PLATE PIE

225g/8oz shortcrust pastry
50g/2oz butter, melted
450g/1lb rhubarb, cut into 1-cm/¹/₂-in sticks
zest of 1 orange, chopped and blanched in boiling water
2 pieces preserved ginger in syrup, chopped
115g/4oz sugar
2 egg yolks
icing sugar, for sprinkling
clotted or whipped cream, to serve

1 Divide the pastry in half, and roll out one half in a circle on a lightly floured board.
2 Brush a 25-cm/10-in pie plate with melted butter, and lay the pastry circle on top. Trim around the edge and brush the pastry with melted butter.
3 Wash and shake nearly dry, then place in the middle of the plate. Sprinkle with the orange peel and ginger, and then with the sugar.

4 Roll out the remaining pastry in a large circle and cut out a 5-cm/2-in circle in the middle.
5 Mix the egg yolks with a little water and use to brush the edges of the base pastry. Lay the second piece of pastry on top and press the edges together to seal. Trim and decorate the edges, using your thumb and fingers.
6 Brush the top with eggwash and sprinkle with icing sugar. Bake the pie in a preheated oven at 240°C, 475°F, Gas Mark 9 for 10 minutes, then reduce the temperature to 180°C, 350°F, Gas Mark 4 for 20 minutes, to cook the rhubarb thoroughly.
7 When cooked, sprinkle the pie with icing sugar and serve with clotted or whipped cream.
SERVES: 4

FRUIT PIES

Of course, you can use any combination of fruit in a plate pie. Here are some ideas for you to try: raspberries and almonds; apples and cinnamon; plums and orange juice; gooseberries and elderflowers; peaches and redcurrants; and pears and nutmeg.

JAM ROLY POLY

225g/8oz plain flour
3 teaspoons baking powder
50g/2oz sugar
115g/4oz chopped fresh suet
milk, to moisten
225g/8oz strawberry jam

1 Mix the flour, baking powder and sugar together in a mixing bowl, then rub in the suet. Use some milk to moisten the mixture and pull the dough together. Leave to rest for 30 minutes.
2 Roll out the dough to a 5-mm/¼-in thick rectangular shape and moisten the edges with water.
3 Warm the jam in a saucepan and spread over the dough, leaving the edges clear. Roll up like a Swiss roll and seal the edges.
4 Dampen a pudding cloth in hot water and wring out. Spread it out and sprinkle lightly with flour.
5 Roll up the pudding in the cloth, tie securely and steam above a pan of simmering water for 2 hours.
6 Open up the cloth and test the pudding. If necessary, re-tie the cloth and cook for a little longer. Serve the Jam Roly Poly hot with custard.
SERVES: 4

BREAD AND BUTTER PUDDING

200ml/8fl oz milk
200ml/8fl oz double cream
1 vanilla pod
3 eggs
115g/4oz sugar
4 tea cakes
25g/1oz butter
25g/1oz raisins
25g/1oz strawberry jam
115g/4oz sugar
icing sugar, for sprinkling

1 Put the milk, double cream and vanilla pod in a saucepan, and bring to the boil.
2 Beat the eggs and sugar together. Pour the milk and cream over the top, strain and leave to stand.
3 Cut the tea cakes in half, horizontally, and butter the cut sides. Lay them in a buttered ovenproof dish, add the raisins and sprinkle with jam.
4 Pour the strained custard over the top, then stand in a roasting pan with water halfway up the sides of the dish.
5 Cook in a preheated oven at 200°C, 400°F, Gas Mark 6 for 30-40 minutes. Sprinkle with icing sugar and serve.
SERVES: 4

PINEAPPLE PUDDING

300g/10oz butter
50g/2oz brown sugar
1 small pineapple, peeled, cored and quartered
few glacé cherries
225g/8oz caster sugar
4 eggs, beaten
175g/6oz self-raising flour
2 teaspoons baking powder
50g/2oz ground almonds
3 tablespoons brandy and/or pineapple juice

1 Melt 50g/2oz of the butter and mix with the brown sugar. Brush around the sides and base of a gratin dish.
2 Arrange the pineapple and cherries in the base of the dish.
3 Cream the sugar and remaining butter, add the beaten eggs, then fold in the flour, baking powder and ground almonds. Thin the mixture with some brandy and/or pineapple juice.
4 Pour into the gratin dish and bake in a preheated oven at 180°C, 350°F, Gas Mark 4 for 45 minutes, until cooked. Turn out and serve.
SERVES: 4

TARTE TATIN

300ml/1/2 pint water
350g/12oz sugar
1 vanilla pod
juice of 1 lemon
2 apples, peeled and cored
115g/4oz butter
225g/8oz puff pastry
icing sugar, for dusting
4 balls of vanilla ice cream

1 Put the water in a saucepan with 225g/8oz of the sugar, the vanilla pod and lemon juice. Bring to the boil, stirring to dissolve the sugar, and make a sugar syrup.

2 Put the apples into the sugar syrup and simmer until just cooked but still firm. Remove the apples, allow to cool and then cut in half from top to bottom.
3 In 4 separate 5-cm/2-in tins, melt 25g/1oz of butter in each. Add 25g/1oz of sugar to each tin, stir well and start to caramelize. In a separate pan, colour the peeled side of the apples in a little butter, and then put them, peeled-side down, into the tins.
4 Roll out the pastry 3mm/1/8in thick and cut out 4 circles, 6cm/2 1/2in in diameter. Lay one piece on each tin and press down lightly.
5 Bake in a preheated oven at 180°C, 350°F, Gas Mark 4, for approximately 15 minutes.
6 Carefully turn out on to 4 hot plates. Dust with icing sugar and serve with ice cream.
SERVES: 4

PLUM JALAISE

225g/8oz puff pastry
450g/1lb Victoria plums
50g/2oz orange marmalade
1 egg, beaten
50g/2oz caster sugar

1 Cut the pastry in half. Roll out into 2 oblongs, 5cm/2in wide by 30cm/12in long.
2 Put one strip onto a dampened baking sheet and brush the edges with water.
3 Stone the plums, cut into quarters and lay down the middle of the pastry. Brush with orange marmalade.
4 Fold the second strip of pastry in half lengthwise. Make a series of slits down the pastry, then unfold and lay the pastry on top of the plums. Seal to the lower layer of pastry.
5 Brush with beaten egg and sprinkle with sugar. Bake in a preheated oven at 200°C, 400°F, Gas Mark 6 for 10 minutes, then lower the temperature to 180°C, 350°F, Gas Mark 4 and bake for a further 20 minutes.
SERVES: 4

Opposite: Pineapple Pudding

BAKED NECTARINES WITH FUDGE SAUCE

4 nectarines, halved and stoned
50g/2oz granulated sugar
4 tablespoons orange juice

FOR THE FUDGE SAUCE:
115g/4oz butter
200g/7oz soft brown sugar
150ml/¹/4 pint double cream

1 Sprinkle the nectarine halves with sugar and pour the orange juice over them.
2 Bake in a preheated oven at 180°C, 350°F, Gas Mark 4 for about 15 minutes, or until tender.
3 Make the fudge sauce. Heat the butter, sugar and cream over very gentle heat until the butter has melted, then bring up to a simmer for 2 minutes, stirring. Serve with the baked nectarines.
SERVES: 4

Note: this sauce is also good served hot with scoops of vanilla ice-cream.

PLUM PANCAKES

8 pancakes (see opposite)
6 plums
115g/4oz butter
50g/2oz sugar
juice of 1 orange
juice of 1 lemon
icing sugar, for sprinkling
clotted cream, to serve

1 Make the pancakes and put to one side and keep warm.
2 Skin the plums, split them in half and take out the stones. Cut them into quarters.

3 Melt 50g/2oz of the butter in a saucepan, add the sugar and stir to colour slightly. Carefully add the orange and lemon juice and boil until reduced.
4 In another pan, melt the remaining butter, add the quartered plums and cook gently until coloured but not overcooked.
5 Warm through the pancakes in the sauce, then spoon the plums on to the pancakes, fold over and arrange on 4 hot plates. Sprinkle the pancakes with icing sugar and serve with clotted cream.
SERVES: 4

PEAR FRITTERS

3 large pears
25g/1oz icing sugar
115g/4oz flour
2 eggs
150ml/¹/4 pint light ale
25g/1oz caster sugar
pinch of grated nutmeg
25g/1oz butter, melted
25ml/1fl oz oil
50g/2oz granulated sugar
double cream, to serve

1 Peel and core the pears and cut into 5-mm/¹/4-in thick slices. Dust them with icing sugar.
2 Sift the flour into a bowl. Break the eggs into the middle, add the ale and mix thoroughly, drawing in the flour from the sides.
3 Beat to a smooth batter, then add the sugar, nutmeg and half of the melted butter. Beat well together and leave to stand for 3 minutes.
4 Heat the oil and the rest of the butter in a frying pan. Dip the pears into the batter and fry on one side until golden. Turn over and fry the other side.
5 Remove the fritters and drain on absorbent kitchen paper. Sprinkle with granulated sugar and serve with double cream.
SERVES: 4

CIDER BAKED APPLES

4 crisp dessert apples
4 tablespoons mixed dried fruit
4 tablespoons honey
4 tablespoons cider

1 Core the apples and, with a sharp knife, score through the skin in a circle all the way round just above the centre.

2 Stand the apples in an ovenproof dish and fill the centres with dried fruit. Drizzle the honey over the top, and pour the cider around them.
3 Bake in a preheated oven at 200°C, 400°F, Gas Mark 6 for 30-40 minutes, until the apples are tender right through.
4 Baste at least once during cooking, spooning the juice into the centre of each apple. They can be eaten hot or cold.
SERVES: 4

PANCAKES

115g/4oz plain flour
pinch of salt
2 eggs
300ml/¹/₂ pint milk
lard for frying

1 Put the flour and salt in a bowl. Break in the eggs and add a little of the milk. Beat well until thoroughly blended.
2 Gradually beat in the milk, a little at a time, until the batter is smooth and free of lumps. If wished, you can make the batter in a food processor instead.
3 Leave the batter to stand for at least 30 minutes before using.
4 Heat a tiny knob of lard in a small frying pan and pour in a little of the pancake mixture. Swirl around the pan, tilting the pan to cover the base. Cook over medium heat until the bottom of the pancake is set and golden brown, then flip the pancake over and cook the other side.
5 Slide out of the pan and keep warm while you cook the remaining pancakes in the same way. Serve with sugar and lemon juice or fill with one of the following fillings.
SERVES: 4

WINTER FRUITS FILLING
Soak some dried apricots, peaches, sultanas and other dried fruit of your choice in some orange juice. Heat through gently and stir in the segments of 1 orange, a sliced banana and a sliced apple. Simmer gently and use to fill the pancakes. Serve sprinkled with icing sugar.

APPLE AND CINNAMON FILLING
Peel, core and slice some apples and stew gently with a little brown sugar until softened. Add some cinnamon, to taste and use as a filling for pancakes.

ICE CREAM AND CHOCOLATE SAUCE FILLING
Fill each pancake with a scoop of vanilla ice cream and fold over into quarters. Pour over a little chocolate sauce and serve immediately.

SUMMER FRUITS FILLING
Take 225g/8oz summer berry fruits, e.g. strawberries, raspberries, sliced peaches, apricots etc. Sprinkle with sugar to taste and 2 tablespoons of fruit liqueur. Set aside for 1 hour to macerate. Whip 225ml/8fl oz double cream and fold in the fruit. Use as a filling for pancakes. Serve sprinkled with icing sugar.

CHOCOLATE COATED STUFFED PEARS

75g/3oz cream cheese
1 heaped teaspoon icing sugar
225g/8oz plain chocolate
150ml/5fl oz double cream
1 tablespoon Amaretto liqueur
6 just-ripe pears, with stalks
juice of 1 lemon

1 Mix together the cream cheese and icing sugar to a consistency that holds its shape but is soft enough to spread. Do not over-beat or it will become runny.

2 Break the chocolate into pieces and melt in a bowl over a pan of barely simmering water. Warm the cream in another bowl over simmering water. Remove the chocolate from the heat, stir until smooth and mix in the warmed cream and Amaretto. Set aside.

3 Peel the pears and cut the bases level so that they will stand upright. Hollow out the core of each pear from the centre of the base. Brush with lemon juice to prevent them discolouring and blot with kitchen paper. Stuff the hollows with the cream cheese mixture.

4 Holding each pear at the top, coat the base with the chocolate mixture. Then holding the pear by the stalk, coat the rest of it so that it is completely covered. Set aside in a cool place until the chocolate sets. Serve each pear decorated with a small leaf, e.g. a bay leaf.
SERVES: 4

Robert Carrier is internationally recognised as a popular and successful food writer and restaurateur. A television presenter and the author of many best-selling cookery books, he was awarded an OBE in 1987 for his services to the field of catering.

DELICIOUS CHOCOLATE DESSERTS

BASIC DARK CHOCOLATE MIX

450g/1lb quality bitter chocolate
grated zest of 1 orange
juice of 2 oranges
50g/2oz butter, diced
1 teaspoon instant coffee
1 teaspoon cocoa powder
4 egg yolks
2 egg whites

1 Break the chocolate into the top of a double boiler, or place in a bowl over a saucepan of water.
2 Add the orange zest and juice to the chocolate, together with the butter, coffee and cocoa powder.
3 Heat the mixture over simmering water, stirring occasionally, until the chocolate has melted. Remove from the heat.
4 Put the egg yolks in a mixing bowl and beat together thoroughly.
5 Strain the chocolate mixture onto the egg yolks through a fine sieve, beating constantly with a hand-held electric whisk, if possible. Allow to cool.
6 In a clean bowl, using a clean whisk, beat the egg whites until stiff, but not dry.
7 Using a spatula, gently but thoroughly, fold the whisked whites into the chocolate/egg mixture. Use to make the following recipes.

PETITS POTS AU CHOCOLAT

1 Add 2-4 tablespoons of orange curaçao (or Grand Marnier) to the basic chocolate mixture and mix well.
2 Stir in a little whipped cream, to taste, and pour into 4 individual 150ml/5fl oz ramekin dishes.
3 Cover and chill in the refrigerator for about 2 hours, until set.
4 Just before serving, cut one thin slice from the centre of an orange and cut the slice into 8 triangles, including the peel. Arrange 2 orange segments on top of each dish.
5 Pour one teaspoon of orange curaçao (or Grand Marnier) over the top of each dish, gently rotating it so that the entire surface is coated. Serve immediately.
SERVES: 4

DARK CHOCOLATE TARTLETS

1 Add 2-4 tablespoons dark rum to the basic chocolate mixture and mix well.
2 Stir in a little whipped cream, to taste, and spoon the mixture into 4 individual baked tartlet shells and leave in a cool place to set.
3 When ready to serve, decorate each little chocolate tart with whipped cream, fresh berries and a sprig of sugared fresh mint.
SERVES: 4

APPLE FOOL

450g/1lb Bramley apples
50g/2oz butter
good pinch of ground cinnamon
pinch of ground nutmeg
caster sugar, to sweeten
2 tablespoons sweet dessert wine
300ml/¹/₂ pint double cream
3 egg yolks
almond biscuits, to serve

1 Peel and core the apples and cut into small pieces. Melt the butter in a large pan, add the apples and spices, and cook gently for about 5 minutes.
2 Crush the apple with a fork and sweeten with sugar, to taste – do not purée. Mix in the dessert wine.
3 Boil the cream, then stir it into the egg yolks and return to the pan. Stir over a low heat until it thickens. Keep stirring all the time and do not allow it to boil. Remove from the heat and cool.
4 When cold, combine the custard with the crushed apple. Serve lightly chilled with almond biscuits.
SERVES: 4

CREAM CROWDIE OR CRANACHAN

50g/2oz medium oatmeal
75ml/3fl oz malt whisky
2 tablespoons thick honey
50g/2oz cream cheese or crowdie
115g/4oz fresh raspberries (or other soft fruit)
150ml/¹/₄ pint double cream
4 teaspoons clear honey

1 Steep the oatmeal in malt whisky and thick honey overnight. Mix in the cream cheese and raspberries.
2 Beat the cream until stiff and put a spoonful in the base

of a wine goblet. Put the oatmeal and honey mixture on top and finish with the remaining cream. Make a slight well in the centre and pour in the clear honey. Repeat with 3 other wine goblets and serve.
SERVES: 4

ICED LIME SOUFFLÉ

3 egg yolks
115g/4oz icing sugar
juice of 2 limes
1 egg white
grated zest of 1 lime
300ml/¹/₂ pint double cream, whipped

1 Beat the egg yolks, sugar and juice of 1 lime in a bowl over a pan of simmering water. Keep beating over gentle heat until foamy, then remove and beat over ice until cold.
2 Whisk the egg white to stiff peaks and fold in to the mixture with the rest of the lime juice and the grated zest. Carefully fold in the whipped cream.
3 Tie some greaseproof paper round 4 individual soufflé dishes to a height of 5cm/2in above the top of the dishes.
4 Pour in the mixture to within 1cm/¹/₂in of the top of the paper. Freeze until set. Remove the paper before serving.
SERVES: 4

Opposite: Apple Fool

QUICK FRUIT SALAD

Prepare some fresh fruits, e.g. strawberries, raspberries, cherries, orange segments, peaches, kiwi fruit, melon, pineapple and mango etc. Put in a large serving bowl and sprinkle with sugar. Pour over some fresh orange juice and 2 tablespoons of fruit liqueur (optional).

LEMON POSSET AND BRANDY SNAPS

300ml/¹/2 pint double cream
150g/5oz sugar
juice of 2 lemons
50ml/2fl oz white wine
1 egg white

1 Put the cream and 115g/4oz of the sugar in a saucepan and bring to the boil. Add the lemon juice and white wine slowly, stirring all the time until it thickens slightly. Remove from the heat and cool.
2 Beat the egg white with the remaining sugar until stiff. Fold into the cream and wine mixture, and pour into 4 individual moulds.
3 Leave to set in the refrigerator. Serve with brandy snaps.
SERVES: 4

BRANDY SNAPS

115g/4oz butter, softened
250g/9oz sugar
250g/9oz golden syrup, warmed
¹/2 teaspoon ground ginger
250g/9oz flour
splash of brandy

1 Cream the butter and sugar and add the warmed golden syrup. Mix in the ginger and flour, and stir in the brandy.
2 Put into a bowl, cover with cling film and leave in the refrigerator until set. Mould into small balls, the size of a hazelnut.
3 Push the balls down onto a baking sheet, 15cm/6in apart. Cook in a preheated oven at 180°C, 350°F, Gas Mark 4 for 5-10 minutes, until golden brown.
4 While they are still warm, wrap the brandy snaps around a greased wooden spoon handle.

BROWN BREAD ICE CREAM

75g/3oz fresh brown breadcrumbs
75g/3oz Demerara sugar
2 eggs, separated
1 tablespoon clear honey
450ml/³/4 pint double cream
2 tablespoons brandy (optional)

1 Mix the breadcrumbs and sugar together. Spread them out on a baking tray, then toast in a preheated oven at 200°C, 400°F, Gas Mark 6. Turn them frequently with a wooden spoon until the sugar melts into the breadcrumbs and looks like a dark, crunchy caramel. Remove from the oven and cool.

2 Beat the egg yolks with the honey in a large bowl. Whisk the cream in another bowl until it just holds its shape. In a third bowl, whisk the egg whites until stiff.
3 Fold the cream into the egg yolk and honey mixture, mixing well. Gently fold in the stiff egg whites.
4 Stir in the cooled sugar and breadcrumb mixture, and the brandy (if using). Spoon into a freezer container and leave in the freezer for several hours or overnight.
5 Remove the ice cream from the freezer and place in the refrigerator to soften a little 20 minutes before serving. This ice cream will keep in the freezer for up to a month.
SERVES: 4

YORKSHIRE CURD TART

225g/8oz shortcrust pastry
115g/4oz sugar
50g/2oz currants
2 eggs, beaten
1/2 teaspoon grated nutmeg

FOR THE CURDS:
600ml/1pint milk
3 beaten eggs
1 teaspoon salt

1 Make the curds. Put the milk, beaten eggs and salt in a saucepan. Bring to the boil, stirring well. Pour into a sieve, lined with muslin, and leave for about 20 minutes, until ready for use.
2 Roll out the pastry and use to line a pie plate.
3 Mix the curds with the sugar, currants and beaten eggs and pour into the lined pie.
4 Sprinkle with grated nutmeg and bake in a preheated oven at 180°C, 350°F, Gas Mark 4 for 20 minutes.
SERVES: 4

FARMHOUSE SYLLABUB

75g/3oz caster sugar
good pinch of grated nutmeg
75ml/3fl oz dry cider
75ml/3fl oz beer
450ml/3/4 pint double cream, whipped

1 Put the sugar, nutmeg, cider and beer in a saucepan and simmer gently for 5 minutes, stirring to dissolve the sugar. Leave to cool completely.
2 Blend with the whipped cream and leave to stand for 1 hour.
3 Pile the syllabub into tall glasses. Leave to separate slightly before serving chilled.
SERVES: 4

KIWI TART

300g/10oz sweet pastry
10 kiwi fruit
200ml/8fl oz double cream, whipped
apricot jam, for glazing

1 Roll out the pastry 3mm/1/8in thick and use to line an 20-cm/8-in flan case. Fill with foil and baking beans and bake 'blind' in a preheated oven at 200°C, 400°F, Gas Mark 6 for 15-20 minutes, until cooked through. Leave to cool.
2 Peel the kiwi fruit and slice 6 of them into rondels. Chop the rest of them up.
3 Whip the cream and mix in the chopped kiwi. Use to fill the flan case and lay the sliced kiwi fruit on top.
4 Put a little apricot jam in a saucepan and bring to the boil. Brush over the kiwi fruit and serve.
SERVES: 4

CHAPTER NINE

CAKES AND BAKING

Everyone enjoys delectable home-made cakes and bread. They take no time at all to prepare and are well worth the effort. You can be sure that your family and friends will appreciate your efforts, and we have a marvellous selection for you to try, ranging from a classic Sachertorte and a prize-winning Chocolate Cake to homely Apple and Yogurt Scones. There are even special recipes for microwave cakes.

Sachertorte (see page 134)

MARMALADE CAKE

450g/1lb mixed dried fruit
250g/9oz self-raising wholemeal flour
pinch of salt
1/2 teaspoon cinnamon (optional)
115g/4oz soft brown sugar
115g/4oz butter or margarine
2 eggs, beaten
3 tablespoons marmalade

1 Put the dried fruit in a bowl, and cover with boiling water. Leave to soak for 1 hour.
2 Put the flour, salt, cinnamon and sugar in a bowl. Add the butter or margarine in pieces, and rub in until the mixture resembles fine breadcrumbs.
3 Add the beaten eggs and marmalade, and mix well. Drain the water off the dried fruit and stir into the mixture.
4 Spoon into a well-greased 20-cm/8-in round cake tin and bake in a preheated oven at 160°C, 325°F, Gas Mark 3 for 1½ hours, or until a skewer inserted into the middle comes out clean.

SACHERTORTE

100g/3½oz quality plain chocolate
115g/4oz slightly salted butter, softened
115g/4oz caster sugar
6 large eggs, separated
115g/4oz plain flour
4 tablespoons apricot jam
whipped cream, to serve

FOR THE ICING:
200g/7oz quality plain chocolate
150ml/1/4 pint double cream
115g/4oz icing sugar

1 Break the chocolate into squares and melt in a bowl over a pan of barely simmering water. Leave to cool a little.

2 Cream the butter with three-quarters of the sugar, then beat in the egg yolks and the cooled, melted chocolate. Fold in the flour.
3 Whisk the egg whites until they form stiff peaks, then fold in the remaining sugar and whisk again. Stir a spoonful into the chocolate mixture, and then fold in the rest with a metal spoon.
4 Pour into a greased and lined 20-cm/8-in round cake tin, and bake in a preheated oven at 180°C, 350°F, Gas Mark 4 for 1-1¼ hours. Leave the cake in the tin for a few minutes before turning out to cool.
5 When cool, cut the cake in half horizontally and sandwich together with apricot jam.
6 Make the icing. Melt the chocolate in a bowl over a pan of simmering water, and allow to cool. Mix into the cream and then stir in the sifted icing sugar.
7 The mixture will thicken as it cools. When it is thick enough to coat the back of a wooden spoon, pour it slowly over the cake, smoothing over the top and sides with a palette knife.
8 If wished, put a little of the icing in a piping bag and pipe 'Sacher' in a flourish across the top. Serve the cake sliced, with whipped cream.

CHOCOLATE CAKE

This recipe by Gabrielle Jackson won the *This Morning Chocolate Cake* competition.

115g/4oz quality plain chocolate
1 tablespoon strong coffee or rum
115g/4oz unsalted butter, softened
115g/4oz caster sugar
3 eggs, separated
pinch of salt
50g/2oz ground almonds
1/4 teaspoon almond extract
50g/2oz plain flour, sifted

FOR THE ICING:
50g/2oz quality plain chocolate
1 tablespoon rum or strong coffee
50g/2oz unsalted butter

FOR THE DECORATION:
toasted, blanched whole almonds
chocolate leaves

1 Melt the chocolate with the coffee or rum in a bowl over a pan of barely simmering water.
2 Cream the butter with all but one tablespoonful of the sugar, until pale and fluffy. Beat in the egg yolks, then blend in the melted chocolate and stir in the ground almonds and almond extract.
3 Beat the egg whites with the salt until they form soft peaks. Add the remaining sugar and beat until stiff peaks form.
4 Fold one-quarter of the egg whites into the chocolate mixture followed by one-quarter of the flour. Continue folding them in until the egg whites and flour are used up.
5 Spoon the mixture into a well-greased and floured 20-cm/8-in cake tin. Bake in a preheated oven at 180°C, 350°F, Gas Mark 4 for 25 minutes, or until well risen and springy to the touch.
6 Allow the cake to cool in the tin for 10 minutes, then run a knife around the edge and turn out on to a wire cooling rack. Leave until thoroughly cold.

7 Make the icing. Melt the chocolate and rum or coffee over some simmering water. Remove the bowl from the hot water and beat in the butter, a tablespoon at a time. Beat the icing over cold water until the mixture is cool and of a spreading consistency.
8 Spread the icing over the cake with a spatula or knife and decorate with the almonds and chocolate leaves.

APPLE, PRUNE AND BROWN SUGAR MUFFINS

115g/4oz plain flour
115g/4oz wholemeal flour
1/2 teaspoon salt
2 teaspoons baking powder
115g/4oz light muscovado sugar
1 large egg
225ml/8fl oz natural yogurt
4 tablespoons sunflower oil
1 large dessert apple, e.g. Golden Delicious
150g/5oz prunes, stoned and chopped
2 tablespoons sunflower seeds

1 Sift the flours, salt and baking powder into a large bowl, adding any bran that remains in the sieve.
2 Stir in the sugar and beat in the egg with the yogurt and oil.
3 Cut the apple into quarters, removing the core and chopping the flesh, and add with the prunes and sunflower seeds to the muffin mixture.
4 Divide the mixture between 12 paper-lined sections of a muffin tin, filling each one about one-quarter full.
5 Bake in a preheated oven at 200°C, 400°F, Gas Mark 6 for 20-25 minutes. Serve warm, split and buttered.
MAKES: 12

Variations: you can substitute other fruits in these muffins, such as blueberries and blackcurrants.

MICROWAVE CAKES

These cakes have been tested on a 750 watt microwave oven, so consult your own microwave oven handbook to adjust, if necessary. As a general rule, go for under rather than over cooking, and remember that standing time will continue the cooking period. Make sure you use glass or microwave-safe plastic containers for baking, as these recipes have a high sugar and fat content which will increase the heat. If in doubt, test by standing a half-full tumbler of water in the baking dish and microwave on HIGH for 1 minute. The water should be hot, but the container cold. If the container (not the water tumbler) is hot, it is not suitable.

FUDGY CHOCOLATE LOAF

175g/6oz margarine or butter
175g/6oz soft dark sugar
3 eggs, beaten
175g/6oz self-raising flour
50g/2oz cocoa powder, sifted
50g/2oz ground almonds
1 teaspoon cinnamon
150ml/¹/₄ pint milk

FOR THE FROSTING:
50g/2oz margarine or butter
4 tablespoons milk
225g/8oz icing sugar, sifted
2 tablespoons cocoa powder, sifted

1 Line the base of a 1-kg/2¹/₄-lb microwave loaf dish with greaseproof paper.
2 Cream the margarine and sugar until light and fluffy, then beat in the eggs. Fold in the flour, cocoa powder, almonds, cinnamon and milk.
3 Spoon into the loaf dish and cover with kitchen paper. Cook on HIGH for 8 minutes.
4 Remove the paper and cook on HIGH for 3 minutes. Cool.
5 To make frosting, place all the ingredients in a bowl and cook on HIGH for 30 seconds.
6 Beat well and cook on HIGH for a further 15 seconds. Beat until smooth and leave to cool.
7 When the loaf is cool, spread the frosting over the top.

◆

CARROT CAKE

115g/4oz soft margarine
115g/4oz caster sugar
115g/4oz self-raising wholemeal flour
115g/4oz grated carrot
50g/2oz walnuts, chopped
¹/₂ teaspoon baking powder
2 eggs, beaten
walnut halves, to decorate

FOR THE ICING:
175g/6oz icing sugar, sifted
75g/3oz butter, softened
grated zest and juice of 1 lemon

1 Beat all the ingredients together except the walnut halves. Spoon into a greased and base-lined 17.5-cm/7-in straight-sided deep dish.
2 Microwave on HIGH for 6 minutes. Stand for 5 minutes, then turn out and allow to cool. Cut in half.
3 Beat the ingredients together until smooth.
4 Sandwich the cake with the icing. Cover with the remaining icing and decorate with walnuts.

LUSCIOUS LEMON CAKE

115g/4oz butter, softened
175g/6oz caster sugar
2 large eggs
175g/6oz self-raising flour
pinch of salt
grated zest of 1 lemon
4 tablespoons milk
strips of lemon zest, to decorate

FOR THE LEMON SYRUP:
75g/3oz icing sugar
juice of 1¹/₂ large lemons

1 Put all the cake ingredients in a large bowl and beat with an electric whisk or a wooden spoon until smooth.

2 Turn into a greased and lined 1kg/2lb loaf tin and smooth the top level. Bake in a preheated oven at 180°C, 350°F, Gas Mark 4 for 45 minutes.

3 Remove from the oven and stand the cake, still in the tin, on a cooling tray.

4 Make the lemon syrup. Heat the sugar and lemon juice gently, stirring to dissolve the sugar, until syrupy.

5 Prick the warm cake all over with a fork and gently pour the syrup over the top. Leave until the cake is cold, then turn out of the tin. Serve sprinkled with icing sugar and thin strips of lemon zest.

Below: Luscious Lemon Cake

PICNIC CAKE

50g/2oz caster sugar
150g/5oz wholemeal self-raising flour
1/4 teaspoon salt
50g/2oz chopped hazelnuts
450g/1lb Bramley apples, peeled and grated
1 large egg
4 tablespoons vegetable oil
225g/8oz cheese, thickly sliced

1 Put the sugar, flour, salt and hazelnuts in a bowl and mix together. Fork the grated apple into the dry mixture.
2 Whisk the egg and oil together, then add to the apple and flour and mix well.
3 Spoon half of the mixture into the base of a greased and lined 17.5-cm/7-in round cake tin and smooth the surface. Lay the sliced cheese on top.
4 Cover with the rest of the cake mixture, and smooth over the surface.
5 Bake in a preheated oven at 180°C, 350°F, Gas Mark 4 for 1^1/$_2$-1^3/$_4$ hours, until firm and springy to the touch in the centre. Allow to cool before taking out of the tin.

———— ◆ ————

HONEY BUNS

225g/8oz wholemeal self-raising flour
pinch of salt
75g/3oz soft brown sugar
75g/3oz butter or margarine
1 large egg
1 tablespoon milk
clear liquid honey
chopped nuts, for sprinkling

1 Put the flour, salt and sugar in a bowl. Add the butter or margarine in pieces and rub until the mixture resembles breadcrumbs.
2 Whisk the egg and milk together and, keeping back just a spoonful to glaze, use to bind the mixture to a soft dough.

3 With floured hands, form into 12 small balls. Place the balls, well spaced out, on 2 small or 1 very large greased baking tray.
4 Make a hole in the top of each ball with a floured finger, and dribble a small teaspoonful of honey into the hole on each bun.
5 Glaze the buns with a pastry brush dipped in the reserved egg and milk mixture, then sprinkle a few chopped nuts over the honey holes.
6 Bake in a preheated oven at 210°C, 425°F, Gas Mark 7 for 10 minutes. Remove from the oven and leave on the tray(s) for a few minutes before cooling on a wire rack.
MAKES: 12

———— ◆ ————

APPLE AND YOGURT SCONES

225g/8oz self-raising flour
50g/2oz polyunsaturated margarine
25g/1oz caster sugar
2 tablespoons desiccated coconut
1 dessert apple, peeled, cored and chopped
150ml/5fl oz natural yogurt

1 Put the flour in a bowl and rub in the margarine. Stir in the sugar, coconut and apple. Mix in the yogurt until you have a soft but not sticky dough. If it is too sticky, add a little flour.
2 Put the dough on a lightly floured board and pat out with the palm of your hand to a round, about 7mm/^{3}/$_4$in thick.
3 Cut the dough into rounds with a plain metal cutter or place the dough on a baking sheet and mark into 8 portions with a knife. Bake in a preheated oven at 220°C, 425°F, Gas Mark 7 for 15-20 minutes (12-15 minutes for smaller rounds). Cool and serve split and buttered.
MAKES: 8

Opposite: Apple and Yogurt Scones

HARVEST BREAD

675g/1¹/₂lb strong bread flour
¹/₂ teaspoon salt
25g/1oz margarine or lard
1 sachet Easy Blend dried yeast
450ml/³/₄ pint hand-hot water

1 Put the flour and salt in a large mixing bowl and rub in the fat. Sprinkle in the yeast and mix thoroughly.
2 Gradually add the water, mixing well with a round-bladed knife until you have a softish dough.
3 Knead the dough on a lightly floured surface for 10 minutes. Place in a lightly oiled bowl, cover with a clean cloth and leave to rise until doubled in volume, about 35-55 minutes depending on the heat of the room.
4 Knock back the dough and shape into loaves, rolls, plaits etc. Here are three ideas for you to try.

ALMOND LOAF

1 Use half the quantity of dough and roll out to a rectangle.
2 Mix together 115g/4oz ground almonds with a lightly beaten egg white and 1 tablespoon sugar. Spread this mixture over the dough and sprinkle with some chopped glacé cherries.
3 Roll up like a Swiss roll and pull the ends round to form a circle. Slash through the surface of the dough at regular intervals. Place on a baking sheet and cover with oiled cling film. Leave to rise for up to 1 hour.
4 Remove the cling film and bake in a preheated oven at 200°C, 400°F, Gas Mark 6 for 30-35 minutes. Cool and then brush with glacé icing and decorate with cherries and flaked almonds.

CHEESE LOAF

1 Roll out the other half of the dough to a rectangle and sprinkle generously with chopped chives and 175g/6oz grated cheese.
2 Roll up the dough like a Swiss roll and either place on a baking tray or in a greased loaf tin. Cover with oiled cling film. Leave to rise for 1 hour.

3 Bake in the preheated oven for 30-35 minutes, and serve warm with soup or salads.

PLAIT

1 Take half the dough and form into a long sausage shape. Make 2 vertical cuts along the length of the dough, leaving it joined at the top.
2 Plait the 3 strands of dough together, place on a baking tray and leave to rise.
3 Bake in the preheated oven for 25-30 minutes. If wished, glaze with a little milk or eggwash and sprinkle with poppy seeds or sesame seeds.

BREADMAKING TIPS

1 Flour: always use a strong bread flour with a high gluten content.
2 Yeast: this causes bread to rise. You can buy it fresh, dried or Easy Blend dried. The Easy Blend variety can be mixed directly into the flour.
3 Salt: this improves the flavour of the loaves. Take care as too much salt can retard the action of the yeast, and too little can cause the dough to rise too fast and produce a crumbly texture.
4 Liquid: water or milk are the usual liquids used in bread-making. Heat, not cold, kills yeast so the liquid must be at the right temperature and never warmer than tepid.
5 Kneading: this strengthens the dough, develops the elasticity of the gluten in the flour and gives a better rise. To knead, fold the dough inwards towards you with one hand while pushing it away from you with the other. Give the dough a quarter-turn and repeat.
6 Rising: the dough should be allowed to rise at least once before baking. It should be covered to keep it moist and warm, and the temperature should be constant. It will take longer at room temperature than in a warm place.

INDEX

Allium tart, 75
Almond loaf, 140
Apple(s),
    and cider, chicken with, 57
    cider baked, 123
    fool, 128
    prune and brown sugar muffins,
        135
    and yogurt scones, 138
Arancini, 58
Arbroath smokie pâté, 110
Aromatic crispy duck, 88
Aubergine bake, Peter Jones's, 71
Bacon,
    ratatouille, 46
    roasted, with lentil and carrot
        stew, 67
Baked field mushrooms, 53
Baked nectarines with fudge sauce,
    122
Baked potato toppings, 61
Baked stuffed mushrooms, 74
Balti spice mix, 90
Balti, vegetable, 90
Basic Balti sauce, 90
Basic white sauce, 71
Bean provencal, 70
Béchamel sauce, 75
Beef,
    in beer, 17
    burgers, 37
        champany, 36
    cobbler, 12
Bobotie, 66
Brandied oranges, 109
Brandy snaps, 130
Bread,
    almond loaf, 140
    and butter pudding, 119

cheese loaf, 140
harvest, 140
plait, 140
Brown bread ice cream, 130
Bruschetta, 34
Bubble and squeak, 20
Burgers,
    beef, 37
        champany, 36
    spicy nut, 36
    tofu, 37
Caesar salad, 52
Cake(s),
    carrot, 136
    chocolate, 135
        loaf, fudgy, 136
    luscious lemon, 137
    marmalade, 134
    picnic, 138
    Sachertorte, 134
Caramelized rice puddings, 115
Carling's stir-fry, 28
Carrot cake, 136
Cauliflower soup, 108
Champany beefburger, 36
Cheese,
    darioles, goat's, 72
    loaf, 140
    potato and spinach pie, 72
Chick pea and bacon soup, 53
Chicken,
    with apples and cider, 57
    chilli, 50
    curry, green, 92
    fajitas, 44
    Jamaican jerk, 85
    lemon and tarragon, 102
    pie, 14
    piri piri, 85

satay, pork and, 84
sauté, 50
teriyaki, 84
Turkish circassian, 56
Chilli chicken, 50
Chilli con carne, 60
Chinese nuts and noodles, 30
Chocolate,
    basic dark mix, 126
    cake, 135
    coated stuffed pears, 124
    petits pots au chocolat, 126
    tartlets, dark, 126
Chops, finger lickin', 46
Cider baked apples, 123
Cod and olive salad, 52
Coleslaw, 80
Cottage pie, quick crunchy, 12
Courgette(s),
    gratin, 74
    and raisin salad, 80
Cowboy baked beans, 60
Cream crowdie or cranachan, 128
Creamy fish pie, 13
Crispy leek and cheese flan, 70
Croque monsieur, 26
Crostini, 34
Cullen skink, 42
Cumberland sauce, 12
Curry, green chicken, 92
Dark chocolate tartlets, 126
Duck, aromatic crispy, 88
Eggs, poached on ham and spinach,
    27
Fajitas, chicken, 44
Farmhouse syllabub, 131
Filo samosas, 26
Finger lickin' chops, 46
Fish pie, creamy, 13

Flan(s),
    crispy leek and cheese, 70
    Moroccan, 48
Fool, apple, 128
Fred's cheesy French toast, 27
Frittata, 27
Fritters, pear, 122
Frying pan pizza, 62
Fudgy chocolate loaf, 136
Gammon with cider, glazed, 17
Glamorgan sausages, 74
Glazed gammon with cider, 17
Goat's cheese darioles, 72
Gratin(s),
    courgette, 74
    dauphinois, 109
Green bean salad, 80
Green chicken curry, 92
Green curry paste, 92
Green pasta with nut sauce, 76
Grilled belly of pork, 64
Grilled mussels, 106
Harvest bread, 140
Hen on her nest, 18
Herby mince and potato pie, 66
Honey buns, 138
Hotpot, Lancashire, 22
Ice cream,
    brown bread, 130
    melon and ginger, 103
Iced lime soufflé, 128
Indonesian soy relish, 84
Indonesian vegetable stew, 86
Irish stew, 23
Italian meat loaf, 44
Jam roly poly, 119
Jamaican jerk chicken, 85
Kedgeree,
    kipper, 56
    Susan's, 40
Kipper kedgeree, 56
Kiwi tart, 131
Lamb,
    finger lickin' chops, 46

shoulder of, with rice and
    apricots, 108
    with spinach, 91
Lancashire hotpot, 22
Lasagne, smoked haddock, 41
Leek and potato soup, 100
Lemon,
    cake, luscious, 137
    and ginger syllabub, 107
    posset and brandy snaps, 130
    pudding, 105
    and tarragon chicken, 102
Lentil salad, 52
Lime soufflé, iced, 128
Luscious lemon cake, 137
Mango chow, 96
Marmalade cake, 134
Meat loaf, Italian, 44
Mediterranean pasta, 40
Melon and ginger ice cream, 103
Mooli relish, 88
Moroccan flan, 48
Muffins, apple, prune and brown
    sugar, 135
Mushroom(s),
    baked field, 53
    baked stuffed, 74
    in red wine, salad of, 104
    stovies with, 80
Mussels, grilled, 106
Nectarines with fudge sauce,
    baked, 122
Norfolk stew and dumplings, 20
Orange(s),
    brandied, 109
Pan fried steaks with Victoria
    plums, 104
Pancakes, 123
    with avocado, sweetcorn, 78
    plum, 122
Parson's venison, 114
Pasta,
    green, with nut sauce, 76
    Mediterranean, 40

penne with chilli sauce, 30
    with pesto, 30
    sesame and broccoli, 76
    smoked haddock lasagne, 41
    tagliatelle with beans and
        ricotta, 76
    triple tomato, 60
    with tuna, 62
Pâté, Arbroath smokie, 110
Pavlova, strawberry and passion
    fruit, 101
Peanut sauce, 85
Pear(s),
    chocolate coated stuffed, 124
    fritters, 122
Penne with chilli sauce, 30
Pesto, pasta with, 30
Peter Jones's aubergine bake, 71
Petits pots au chocolat, 126
Pheasant,
    with chestnuts and sprouts,
        roast, 18
    with wild mushrooms, roast, 110
Picnic cake, 138
Pie(s),
    cheese, potato and spinach, 72
    chicken, 14
    creamy fish, 13
    herby mince and potato, 66
    rhubarb plate, 118
Pineapple pudding, 120
Pizza, 32
    frying pan, 62
Plum(s),
    jalaise, 120
    pan fried steaks with Victoria,
        104
    pancakes, 122
Poached eggs on ham and
    spinach, 27
Polentini, 81
Pork,
    and chicken satay, 84
    fillet Cordon Bleu, 106

grilled belly of, 64
red hot ribs, 47
alla Romana, 37
Potato(es),
    pancakes, 78
    toppings, baked, 61
Prawn(s),
    salad of warm, 114
    soup, spicy, 86
    sweet and sour, 88
Quick crunchy cottage pie, 12
Ratatouille, bacon, 46
Red hot ribs, 47
Rhubarb plate pie, 118
Rice puddings, caramelized, 115
Richard's tuna casserole, 67
Roast pheasant with chestnuts
    sprouts, 18
Roast pheasant with wild
    mushrooms, 110
Roasted bacon with lentil and
    carrot stew, 67
Saag gosht, 91
Sachertorte, 134
Salad(s),
    caesar, 52
    cod and olive, 52
    courgette and raisin, 80
    green bean, 80
    lentil, 52
    of mushrooms with red wine, 104
    of warm prawns, 114
Salmon,
    en croûte with a spinach filling,
        100
    pattie cakes, 36
Samosas, filo, 26
Satay, pork and chicken, 84
Sauce(s),
    basic Balti, 90

basic white, 71
béchamel, 75
Cumberland, 12
dipping, 94
peanut, 85
tasty meat, 13
tomato and basil, 58
Sausage(s),
    cakes and herby toad, 14
    in cider, 64
    Glamorgan, 74
Scallops with green mango, 102
Scones, apple and yogurt, 138
Scotch broth, 40
Sesame and broccoli pasta, 76
Shoulder of lamb with rice and
    apricots, 108
Skate with black butter sauce, 112
Smoked bacon and cabbage, 16
Smoked haddock lasagne, 41
Snapper with calaloo, 96
Soufflé, iced lime, 128
Soup(s),
    cauliflower, 108
    chick pea and bacon, 53
    cullen skink, 42
    Scotch broth, 40
    leek and potato, 100
    spicy crunchy tomato, 43
    spicy prawn, 86
Spanish omelette, 26
Spicy crunchy tomato soup, 43
Spicy nut burgers, 36
Spicy prawn soup, 86
Spring rolls with a dipping sauce, 94
Steak(s),
    and kidney pudding, 16
    pan fried, with Victoria plums,
        104
Stew of fennel and tomatoes, 78

Sticky toffee pudding, 118
Stir-fry, Carling's, 28
Stovies with mushrooms, 80
Strawberry and passion fruit
    pavlova, 101
Sweet and sour prawns, 88
Sweetcorn pancakes with
    avocado, 78
Susan's kedgeree, 40
Syllabub,
    farmhouse, 131
    lemon and ginger, 107
Tabbouleh, 71
Tagliatelle with beans and ricotta,
    76
Tart(s),
    allium, 75
    kiwi, 131
    Yorkshire curd, 131
Tarte citron, 111
Tarte tatin, 120
Tartlets, dark chocolate, 126
Tasty meat sauce, 13
Teriyaki chicken, 84
Toast toppings, 34
Tofu burgers, 37
Tomato(es),
    and basil sauce, 58
    pasta, triple, 60
    soup, spicy crunchy, 43
Tortilla, 26
Triple tomato pasta, 60
Tuna,
    casserole, Richard's, 67
    pasta with, 62
Turkish circassian chicken, 56
Vegetable Balti, 90
Venison steaks with Stilton, 20
White sauce, basic, 71
Yorkshire curd tart, 131